How to
IDENTIFY & MANAGE RISK IN GLOBAL MARKETS

INVESTORS
PRESS

Published in the United States by Investors Press, Inc.

Library of Congress Cataloging-in-Publication Data
    Investors Press, Inc.
    How To Identify & Manage Risk In Global Markets
        ISBN-1-885123-14-0
        I. How To Identify & Manage Risk In Global Markets

Printed in the United States
10   9   8   7   6   5   4   3   2   1

Book and jacket design by Silver Communications Inc., NYC.

ACKNOWLEDGEMENT

Investors Press is pleased to present **How To Identify & Manage Risk In Global Markets.**

Each book in our ongoing Investment Management Series examines important issues of compelling concern to pension and investment officers, trustees, benefits administrators, pension consultants and money managers. Written by distinguished plan sponsors, trustees and industry professionals, each chapter reflects their individual experience and offers the author's independent opinions and informed insights.

Published by Investors Press, this unique educational series is made possible by the support and participation of a select group of leading firms to whom appreciation goes from everyone who values the importance of education and the candid exchange of information. Because of their commitment, these books are valuable tools that encourage industry-wide dialogue, discussion and deeper understanding.

INVESTORS PRESS

How to
IDENTIFY & MANAGE RISK IN GLOBAL MARKETS

Underwritten by

ALTERNATIVE INVESTMENT MANAGEMENT ASSOCIATION (AIMA)

BANKERS TRUST COMPANY - RAROC 2020^{SM}

CHICAGO MERCANTILE EXCHANGE

DELAWARE GROUP

FIDELITY MANAGEMENT TRUST COMPANY ("FMTC")

FIRST UNION NATIONAL BANK

HOLL INTERNATIONAL LLC

INDEPENDENCE INVESTMENT ASSOCIATES, INC. AND SUBSIDIARY

INSTINET CORPORATION

JOHN HANCOCK

METLIFE

MORGAN GRENFELL ASSET MANAGEMENT LTD.

ROGERS, CASEY & ASSOCIATES, INC.

TABLE OF CONTENTS

INTRODUCTION

After registering years of mediocre returns, global equity investors remind themselves that patience is indeed a virtue. Many pioneers of the early 1980s pursued opportunities in the global markets using a return-based approach; they focused on relatively few stocks and equally few countries. As the decade drew to a close, they watched the market evolve to a more exposure-based approach as virtually all U.S. pension funds dove in to add a global component to their portfolios.

The global markets, once considered the plan sponsor's instant diversification tool, now require strategic maneuvering of correlation and liquidity risks. As developed markets around the world increasingly move in sync with one another, equity market performance is not materially different outside of the U.S., as it had been over the last 15 years.

When savvy pension funds turn to less-developed markets to seek diversity, they face other risks, such as liquidity risk, which in theory should diminish as market participation increases, but in practice does not because those markets are in actuality dependent on large investments made by a relatively small number of institutions. Ironically, the apparent increase in liquidity, often deceptive, is accompanied by a much greater risk of significant short-term correlation.

With all the complexities of the global markets—less than stellar returns, correlation, liquidity, currency and political risks—plan sponsors ask themselves if it does it in fact make sense to hang one more, personal career risk, in the balance of plan performance?

Certainly, to ignore or decrease your exposure in global markets is not the answer. When a large percentage of the world's market capitalization lies outside U.S. boundaries, the prudent answer is to identify and manage risks in various global markets with skill and agility.

There is not, however, one distinct risk management strategy for domestic investing and another for global investing. Often, plan sponsors believe that a significantly different skill set is required to master the global markets. While it is true that there are special considerations to be made when your portfolio travels abroad—most notably currency issues—more and more plan sponsors are developing comprehensive risk management programs that are truly global in scope and do not isolate domestic investing.

But as this book's Roundtable discussion among four prominent plan sponsors points out, global risk measurement is an area where one size does not fit all. The needs of John Lawson in running the single, public plan of the Police Department of Houston are very different from those of Desmond Mac Intyre, who monitors risk for multiple corporate plans at General Motors Investment Management Corporation. The liquidity requirements and liability structure faced by Larry Siegel at the Ford Foundation differ from those Robert Spooner considers when he models how various market conditions can affect Eastman Kodak.

Despite that caveat, and the vastly different risk management needs among plans of all shapes and sizes, there are commonalities in approaches to risk measurement and risk management. Indeed, the newsworthy Risk Standards Working Group is founded on this belief. Their proposed industry standards, carefully crafted to help plan sponsors identify, understand, measure and monitor risks, attempt to give plan sponsors a structure for developing sorely needed risk management programs. This distinguished group of plan sponsors and consultants has poured the risk management foundation for their peers; plan sponsors now have firm footing to architect and customize programs and systems for their individual plan structures.

In the first Investors Press chapter written by a non-U.S. plan sponsor, Theo Jeurissen, Managing Director of Strategic Investment Policy, and Fons Quix, Manager, Control, ABP in Holland, provide a case study that describes the early development stages of a global risk program. ABP, the fund covering all government employees in Holland, is governed by trustees who do not have a great deal of financial sophistication, as is often the case at even the largest funds. Until very recently, ABP had been strictly limited in its ability to invest outside of the country. Because the fund is half the size of the entire Dutch stock market, it has been invested 90% in bonds since it is too big to make significant equity investments in such a small market.

In 1996 the fund was set free to invest more widely outside of Holland, a dramatic change and opportunity with enormous political and bureaucratic implications. Readers on both sides of the ocean will gather invaluable wisdom from ABP's story of how it is educating its board about modern portfolio theory, upgrading its risk control department and elevating its pension fund administrators from "bureaucrat" to portfolio management peer status.

In his chapter on "Choosing the Global Risks that Work for You," Michael deMarco, Risk Manager and U.S. Equity Co-Manager, GTE Investment Management, considers underperformance his fund's fundamental risk. GTE believes the key to performance is asset allocation and the key to asset allocation is diversity. Readers will delve deeply into GTE's twofold risk management strategy. They will learn how GTE directs its fund managers to use a wide variety of investing styles and strategies, and utilizes extensive modeling to ensure that GTE is monitoring and, if possible, predicting correlation patterns in the global marketplace.

The question of "Currencies: To Hedge or Not to Hedge?" is posed by Richard

Rose, Chief Investment Officer, San Diego County Employees Retirement Association, as he acknowledges that currency risk has become a major headache for plan sponsors. Rose and his colleagues have found an answer to the problem of how to reduce overall portfolio risk through diversification into international securities: they have transformed a currency hedge designed to remove risk into a value-added strategy designed to seek profits.

Readers will gain insights to the San Diego technique responsible for adding 242 basis points, annualized, to their return on non-U.S. equity in its first two years of operation. Rose feels their new brand of currency management can be replicated by any plan sponsor with more than 5% to 10% of its assets invested in non-U.S. equities.

Craig Scholl, Manager, Asset Allocation and Administration, Hewlett-Packard Company, observes that most investors look for a single risk measure that completely expresses a global portfolio's return risk. He argues that there is no one right risk number and his chapter on "The Benchmark Dilemma: Managing the Hidden Risks" encourages readers to dig below the surface of returns by developing a comprehensive risk profile, a framework for evaluating, discussing and mitigating risks. Scholl postulates that risk is a concept that is frequently talked about, generally understood and often mis-measured—fodder for his focus on the challenges inherent in simply measuring performance relative to a market index.

Some of the most highly regarded pension funds—the giants who dominate global markets and impress their peers with dynamic investment strategy—are curiously lacking in their risk management expertise. Risk management has always been an important part of the plan sponsor's daily responsibilities, but the task has grown in size and significance and the growing pains are shared by plans around the globe.

Through our Roundtable programs and Reader Fax Surveys, plan sponsors repeatedly tell us that an ongoing global risk management dialogue among their peers is an essential learning, investment and management tool. **How to Identify & Manage Risk in Global Markets** is a valuable educational resource that offers risk management **"Smart Pills"** from plan sponsors who continue to grow in skill and in step with the growth of their plans.

The Editors of Investors Press

CHAPTER ONE

A EUROPEAN APPROACH TO GLOBAL RISK MANAGEMENT

Theo Jeurissen, Managing Director, Strategic Investment Policy
Fons Quix, Manager, Control
ABP (Dutch Government Pension Fund)

At ABP, the Dutch Government Pension Fund, change is coming very fast. In 1996 we became an independent plan, released for the first time from the regulation of the Ministry of Finance. This new freedom has allowed us to make dramatic shifts in our asset allocation, spurred by increasing competitive challenges and an European economic integration that will ultimately yield a single currency. We have shifted from buy-and-hold to active management, accepting all the cultural changes that implies. All these changes, challenges and opportunities make stringent risk management and risk controls more necessary than ever. But an even greater challenge is giving the Board and the entire organization the knowledge and comfort level they need to embrace new investment risks and opportunities.

ABP is the pension fund for all public employees in the Netherlands. We have about a million people paying into the fund and our assets under management are 250 billion guilders, about $125 billion. As an independent plan, we are now subject to the Pensions and Savings Act that governs all pension plans in the Netherlands; previously, we had been subject to a law and accompanying regulation that regulated only ABP. Under it, the Ministry of Finance effectively determined our asset allocation, as well as many of our other investment decisions.

INCREASED COMPETITION

In Holland we have the same three-tier system that exists in the United States: our equivalent of the American Social Security system, defined benefit pension plans and defined contribution plans. No individual can take money out of one tier and put it into another.

As a result of changes to the system, however, beginning in 2001, sectors, such as teachers or the police force, currently covered by ABP, will be able to take their pension plans to other providers. The details of how this will work have not been decided, but the approaching changes have already made the pension industry much more competitive and this competition will increase. We will be competing

2:45 p.m.

You've just been assigned the task to liquidate a global portfolio. How do you access liquidity and knowledge of local markets in over 30 countries?

INSTINET

Instinet is a global agency broker, helping securities industry professionals reduce transaction costs through best execution and the innovative application of advanced computer and communications technology. Through Instinet, you get access to equity trading opportunities in the U.S. and more than 30 countries worldwide plus proprietary research and trading tools that help you perform at your best.

INSTIN∷T®

A REUTERS Company

The Power to do More

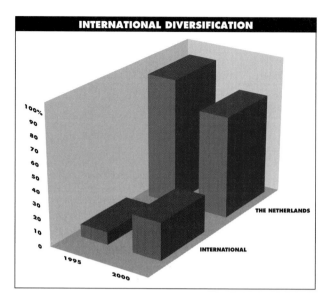

INTERNATIONAL DIVERSIFICATION

100% 90 80 70 60 50 40 30 20 10 0

THE NETHERLANDS

INTERNATIONAL

1995   2000

not just with insurance companies, but with banks, to hold on to our current beneficiaries and attract individual savings, as well.

These challenges put pressure on us to market ourselves more effectively. In a competitive market, image becomes much more of an issue—and we have not been perceived as a very dynamic company. Because we have been regulated by the government, we are seen as bureaucratic. We expect that a shift from our traditional buy-and-hold management approach toward active management will help to change our image.

In addition to these industry changes, we have to deal with the fundamental economic sea change going on in Europe. Although there is occasional hesitance about a single European currency, our view is that it will succeed. Once that happens, we will treat all of Europe as our home market, and move a much greater proportion of our investments outside the Netherlands.

DRAMATIC SHIFTS IN ASSET ALLOCATION

Independence has already changed our asset allocation considerably. Before January 1996, the unique set of laws and regulations that applied only to us didn't explicitly control our asset allocation, but they put such strict limits on the amount we could invest in various markets that they might as well have controlled it. There were, effectively, no choices available; we had to buy and hold whatever we could invest in. Now we are moving from a world without choices to a world full of choices.

Those regulations led to an allocation where ABP had 90% of its assets in fixed-income, mainly invested in the Netherlands. Though we would have liked to have had more equity, our equity exposure was also effectively limited to the Dutch market. Because we are such a large fund, our buying more equity would have had an enormous effect on the Dutch market. Eventually, we convinced the Ministry of Finance that restricting us to the Netherlands was an outdated concept. They gave us some leeway—first 5% and then 10%—for investments abroad. That gave us the opportunity to gain some experience in investing worldwide.

Now, on the basis of asset-liability studies, we are aiming at an asset allocation of 30% equity, 10% real estate and 60% fixed-income by the year 2000. Currently, our equity exposure is about 20% of our total investments, already a significant increase, and we're aiming at a much bigger exposure in equity worldwide. But, partly because of the way we calculate our premiums, we have to move gradually.

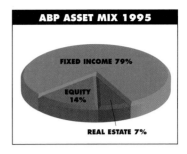

When our coverage ratio is too low, we have to raise the premiums we charge plan sponsors. Obviously, the plan sponsors don't like this and one way we avoid it is not to lower premiums quickly. When our equity and real estate investments increase in value, we hold the first 30% increase in value as a cushion; we don't lower premiums until the market value has moved above that. New investments, obviously, don't

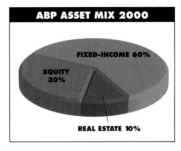

have that cushion. If we moved quickly to boost our equity allocation, our cushion would shrink. If the market dropped, we would have to raise premiums.

UPDATING RISK CONTROL

The changes around us are having a dramatic effect on more than just our asset allocation. They are forcing us to look much harder at the way we manage and control risk. Because operating successfully within this new freedom requires reevaluating and revising our systems, the Board of Directors asked an accounting firm in the Netherlands to do a complete audit of the investment department. It concluded that our investment and control processes were sufficient for the management style we had been using, but recommended that we make changes if we wanted to move into more products and markets.

We have a top-down investment process that starts with an asset-liability model. That's our highest level of risk management and we manage risk on both the asset and the liability sides. The liabilities of the fund determine the appropriate asset allocation. Next comes the country allocation, then a series of investment decisions and finally, the portfolio manager who selects the stocks. Within that top-down process, we try to move responsibility and accountability as deeply into the organization as possible—one of the main reasons we pay so much attention to risk control.

We realized that as we moved toward a more complex structure of portfolios, we would need to be able to see the interaction between the risks we were taking across asset classes. Using a non-coordinated reporting system, it was hard to see those risks clearly. For instance, we have an allocation risk that comes from deciding on fixed-income or equity. We have a selection risk that derives from individual stock or debt instrument selection. These risks interact with each other; in a top-down process it's essential to see these different types of risk in an integrated way.

We chose to focus on installing an overall risk control tool. We wanted to link our different systems and, by linking them, provide insight into aggregated plan risk. It was important to see the active risk correlations between our different portfolios and consider them in calculating our overall risk.

STICKING WITH WHAT WE KNOW

When it came to selecting a supplier, we turned to the company that already provides the risk analysis tools we use for portfolio management, rather than ask for bids from other companies. This is a highly regarded company and we have been very satisfied with their past service. We know and trust them and reasoned that since our portfolio managers are already using their software, the transition would be much easier if we stayed with them—provided they could meet our current needs.

Having explained that we wanted a system on which we could put our whole portfolio and see our overall risk exposure, we learned they were developing such a tool, which has now been completed. We are currently implementing it here and expect it to be fully operational shortly. This is an integrated system, fed by the risk management systems within our equity and fixed-income departments. It is a complicated process because the whole portfolio has to be put into a set of models, but it will give us, among many other things, the active risk of the total portfolio, measured by standard deviation from a benchmark.

INTRODUCING MODERN RISK MANAGEMENT CONCEPTS TO THE BOARD

Introducing this system has not been without its stresses and strains, especially given the other challenges our company faces. We have launched a thorough educational process, beginning with the Board and moving downward, throughout the organization.

Our Board members represent employers and union members; we have an independent chairman. None are professional investors and we have never, until now, asked them to look at active risk. Traditionally, risk management has been auditing and establishing basic guidelines on an aggregate level. These guidelines, along with other factors, represent a classic approach to risk management.

Modern risk management, however, laden with concepts like the volatility of specific instruments, the bets we're taking, our exposure and benchmarks, is not familiar to the Board and by introducing these concepts, we don't want to confuse them. If we tell them 25% of our portfolio is now actively managed, they know what we're talking about. But if we tell them we used to have a 1% deviation from the benchmark, and now it's 1.1%? Well, they know that 1.1% is bigger than 1%, but it's a lot more difficult for them to judge what the increase means. So, as we move into modern risk management, we have to make our description of how the investment professional's mind works, how he handles problems, clear and easily understandable to our Board.

The Board is not there to be better investment professionals than we are; that is not their role. But they do have the final accountability for our investment decisions and they have to be able to assume that responsibility. The Board gets our strategic investment plan, our annual plan and quarterly updates that describe what we're doing, how we will allocate investments, what the expectations are behind specific preferences. We try to give them consistent insight into our investment decisions.

The Board also gets information from our investment committee, made up of external professionals. This committee's main job is to advise management on overall investment policy, but it also shares information with the Board. We have an agreement that whenever they want to, they will make their opinions known to the Board either by writing a letter or sending notes of a meeting.

We also make presentations to the Board on different topics; these presentations usually last half a day, occasionally all day. Several have been about derivatives, including an explanation of the use of swaps and a description of the framework for our own use of derivatives. We've also covered asset-liability management, addressed our new risk management approach and submitted a written timetable for seeing initial results.

One of the important issues we've had to deal with is vocabulary. Investment professionals, for instance, might say equity has a 10% return and an 18% standard deviation; that's their way of explaining its risk. But the Board is used to asking what the impact on our coverage ratio is, and to what extent the premium can be affected. For them, that's the relevant way to look at risk.

When we presented an update on our asset-liability management, we included probabilities. Presenting concepts from the world of statisticians in the context of something the Board already understands helps it accept those concepts. It helps members know they're not gimmicks—they have real relationships with coverage ratios and premium volatility. Eventually, we expect that Board members will be able to understand statistics and the corresponding trade-offs in decision-making themselves.

Generally, we give a presentation and then the Board asks questions. We know that no one, and certainly not a member of our Board, wants to sit and listen all day. The presentation is the just starting point and we are willing to be interrupted after five minutes to discuss the issue. We prepare an agenda, but there's a lot of discussion and in some cases we don't get to every point it lists.

These presentations are very much appreciated by members of the Board because they give them the opportunity to gain a basic knowledge and ask questions in an informal setting. Their role, after all, is to ask questions and evaluate the answers, to look at the consistency of how we answer questions and the attitude that underlies the answers. They are very well able to form an opinion on what we are doing without being investment professionals; the presentations help them gain confidence in our decision-making process.

As a result of our efforts, we have also noticed a growing appetite for this kind of information; Board members want to spend more time at it and where they used to "rubber-stamp" our annual reports, there is now much more active involvement from the Board in helping us prepare them.

THE STRESS OF CHANGE

Another target of our educational efforts is our own staff. They are under considerable pressure right now, not only because of the new system, but because of our need to manage actively and attract other customers outside the pension fund. One thing we stress is that we're not centralizing, but integrating. Every portfolio manager still has the responsibility for controlling risks in his portfolio. No one can take that responsibility away from him or make changes in his portfolio.

But as we develop an integrated risk management system, some of those portfolios will have to change. The way we develop portfolios is to have managers make proposals to the directors of the investment department that include specific styles, characteristics, risk parameters and limits. Management either accepts the proposal or asks for adjustments, and the risk parameters are set before any portfolio manager can start to run a portfolio.

As we integrate our risk management, we realize some risk parameters will no longer make sense. Management will either have to change the parameters or invite people to develop new proposals that account for the conflict. This is, in fact, one of the things we hope will happen.

Moving to integrated risk management is also forcing us to upgrade our risk control department and that involves still more education. This is a problem faced throughout the Dutch financial world. The banking sector, for instance, has been experiencing the same problems in its back office. We now require portfolio managers to have in-depth post-graduate courses in finance and be certified financial analysts. To keep the balance, we must now make sure the people working on the control side are as skilled as the portfolio managers, otherwise the whole structure can fall apart. Finding an adequate staff is a problem; here, risk control is a young field of activity.

To ensure a balance between the people controlling risk and the people managing it, all have to be equally skilled and respected. That's something we're working hard on. Part of it is teaching the risk control people to stand up for themselves. Previously, they saw themselves as facilitators and hesitated to make demands on the portfolio managers.

Another issue moving to the forefront is the role of our external portfolio managers and custodians. Currently, our international investment portfolio is almost completely externally managed, although we are moving more toward internal management. Ideally, the information flow from the external managers should be almost the same as from the internally managed portfolio. If we put pressure on the internal managers to get us information on a daily basis, we should put the same pressure on external managers. Integrated information is the basis for integrated risk control. Today, however, we're getting that information primarily from our custodians, who are a key part of our risk control structure.

THE NEW RISK MANAGEMENT SYSTEM: BENEFITS FOR HEDGING

We expect the new system to be very useful in the area of derivatives and hedging. Our policy is to hedge currency exposures; our view is that there's no investment return related to holding currencies. It is possible to have a return, but we don't believe you can have specific return expectations for currencies the way you can for other investments. If you're in fixed-income, you have an interest rate. If you're in equity, you may not be able to predict the precise return, but you know there will be one. There is no sure return on currencies.

We don't hedge, however, to the full extent of our exposure. That's inefficient because there's always a compensating element in the portfolio for the effects of currency devaluation—a country with a weakening currency, for instance, gets a better export position. Generally, we hedge between 40% and 60% of our equity exposure.

Why we at the Delaware Group think we are an investment manager for the times ahead

The Delaware Group, based in Philadelphia, is a large, full-service investment-management firm that invests more than $38 billion on behalf of institutions and individuals. Our institutional division, Delaware Investment Advisers, manages more than $16 billion in separately managed accounts. An overseas counterpart, Delaware International Advisers Ltd., located in London, manages more than $5 billion in separate accounts of global and foreign stocks and bonds.

Investment approach

Our investment approach is designed to *produce consistent, steady returns without corresponding levels of risk, or volatility, over the long term.* We seek to construct portfolios that fluctuate less—that is, portfolios that control volatility more effectively, particularly in declining markets—than those of our institutional peers. We believe strongly that achieving relatively good performance in bear markets is critical to preserving the capital created in bull markets.

As we see it, excessive volatility is not at all conducive to serving our clients well and building their wealth. For instance, if a $10,000 stock portfolio goes up 60% one year but then declines 40% the next, it's worth $9,600 at the end of two years—a loss despite the dazzling performance in the first year (see **Consistency counts**). In contrast, if another $10,000 portfolio rises 30% the first year but drops only 10% the second, that less-volatile portfolio has $11,700 after two years.

Refined over seven decades, our investment approach involves assessing securities, industry sectors, and markets via rational, quantifiable, tested standards of value, such as stock and bond yields, price ratios, and future dividend-income streams. Our approach disciplines us to purchase securities at reasonable prices—a margin of safety so critical to controlling risk. And it provides a disciplined, systematic framework for determining when securities are no longer fairly valued, in our estimation, and should be sold.

Consistency counts: *steady performance—a hallmark of Delaware's investment approach—is invariably superior to widely fluctuating returns in creating wealth*

Growth of $10,000

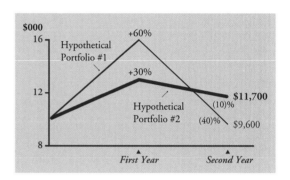

We believe an approach such as ours is well suited for the years ahead. The capital markets have been uncommonly bountiful over the most recent 10-year period, from 1987 through 1996: stocks have compounded at a rate of 15.3% annually (more than four percentage points above the historical average) and intermediate-term government bonds have returned 7.7% (2.4 percentage points better than the long-term average). The next 10 years may not be nearly so kind, may bring weaker bull markets and more severe bear markets. In that kind of environment, low volatility and consistent performance will matter enormously.

Organization

Delaware was founded in 1929 as an investment counseling service employing less than 30 people. Our staff now numbers more than 800, who are responsible for the stewardship of more than 500,000 institutional and mutual-fund client relationships. In April 1995 Delaware was acquired by Lincoln National Corporation, a diversified financial-services company with more than $6.6 billion in annual revenues.

Portfolio management

About 50 investment professionals share the responsibility of managing our portfolios. We believe the best investment decisions are made collectively, so decision-making for each of our portfolios is delegated to a specific team of professionals. We believe such teamwork enhances the process of portfolio management.

13 institutional portfolios

Our 13 customized institutional portfolios of U.S. and foreign stocks and bonds can accommodate clients' differing tolerances for risk and differing needs for capital growth and income (see **Globe-spanning services**). In addition, we offer investment-advisory services, retirement-plan services, and nuclear decommissioning and Voluntary Employee Benefit Association trusts.

Globe-spanning services: *Delaware offers customized portfolios invested in the major asset classes of the world's capital markets and designed to provide various levels of risk/reward potential*

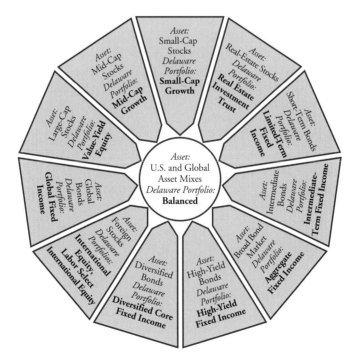

DELAWARE GROUP

One Commerce Square, Philadelphia, Pennsylvania 19103 Telephone (215) 255-2300
Veritas House, 125 Finsbury Pavement, London, England EC2A 1NQ Telephone 011-44-171-638-2493

"We told you never, ever to use that 4-letter word R-I-S-K. For your punishment, four weeks without CNN and an 85% allocation to fixed-income.

We have on occasion taken bets on major currencies like British pounds and the U.S. dollar. In extreme circumstances, when they go to the low or high side of the band, we have deliberately decided on a lower ratio than 50%. 1995 was one of those occasions: the dollar was 1.60 to the guilder. We went down to about 33% and, at one point, as low as 25%.

We do use swaps and futures to manage other positions. We're so large that when we use derivatives, we have to take a sizable position to have any effect. Our Board has been somewhat reluctant on this point, an important reason we've paid a lot of careful attention to how we use them. We use plain vanilla instruments that are much easier to control from a risk control point of view than swaptions, as an example.

Our use of derivatives can be both strategic and tactical. As a strategic policy, we want to hedge our currency exposure, so we use currency swaps. Since the markets change every day, if we want to hold on to a specific strategic position, the underlying drift of markets means we have to rebalance and we use futures for that. In the field of tactical allocation, if we want to underweight the Dutch equity market temporarily because of our short-run return expectations, we sell futures. On an overall basis, we will change our position by using swaps and futures. The new system is going to be very useful in helping us see our overall position more accurately and giving us clearer insight into when to make adjustments in our position.

It goes without saying, perhaps, that a risk measurement system must be able to include derivatives, and that they must be linked to their underlying investments so that we can look at our integrated economic exposure. It's also important to remember that a risk management system, however sophisticated, is only one tool in an overall, integrated risk control strategy.

Even the best risk management system has its limits. The emerging competitive environment, for instance, does present one problem for which we can expect little or no help from our new system. With financial institutions increasingly competing for the customers' funds, there's an increasing appetite in the media for financial information. We, like other financial institutions, are coming under a lot of pressure to give the financial press and the news media, in general, our predictions on financial trends.

Until a few years ago, we had the luxury of taking a scientific approach, saying that it's very difficult or even impossible to predict what the dollar, for instance, will do. But now everyone else in the industry predicts what the dollar will do in three months, six months, a year. And with the whole industry around us putting out these views, we will have to start to do so, too. The risk of embarrassment is one we haven't yet found a system to manage!

 S M A R T   P I L L S

➤ Don't look so hard for the perfect solution that you lose sight of political realities. All other things being equal, or even close to equal, it makes sense to choose the risk management option that will cause the least disruption within your organization.

➤ Remember that the Board of Directors' role is not to manage the investment process; Board members don't need to learn every nuance of Modern Portfolio Theory. They do need to learn enough so they can understand what you're doing and gauge your competence to do it.

➤ Don't be foolish enough to think you can cope with overall risk just by introducing risk measurement systems. You also have to pay attention to organizational structures and, within those structures, to separation of responsibilities, staff expertise and clear objectives and guidelines.

CHOOSING THE GLOBAL RISKS THAT WORK FOR YOU

Michael deMarco, Risk Manager and U.S. Equity Co-Manager
GTE Investment Management

F or GTE, the fundamental risk is the risk of underperformance. Because we
are substantially over-funded, we don't have to worry about a shortfall, and
while we are obviously concerned about losing money in individual portfolios,
that's not where we focus our attention on a global basis. Our horizon is very long-
term; fundamentally, we're not unduly concerned about short-term ups and downs.

Performance is key. We believe the key to performance is asset allocation and
the key to asset allocation is diversity. We try to use every security market globally: all the fixed-income and all the equity markets. Overall, about a third of our
portfolio is invested outside the United States.

Contrary to popular belief, however, investing in multiple markets doesn't
assure diversity. Pension fund managers who think it does are forgetting about two
substantial problems: correlation risk and liquidity risk. Correlation risk is the risk
that markets you expect to move differently will move in sync. In fact, developed
markets around the world tend to do just that. If you look at the differences in
returns between countries in the Morgan Stanley Capital International EAFE
index, for instance, and remove the effects of currency shifts, you'll see that over
the past 15 years, those countries' local equity market performance wasn't materially different from the U.S. equity market's performance. All the diversification
that institutional investors thought they were getting came through the currency
bets they were making.

If, on the other hand, we turn to less-developed markets for diversity, we run
into different risks. Liquidity risk, which in theory should diminish as market participation increases, often does not because those markets are frequently driven by
large investments made by a relatively small number of institutions. Ironically,
that apparent increase in liquidity, often deceptive, is accompanied by a much
greater risk of significant short-term correlation. Mexico's peso devaluation, as an
example, produced what seemed to be an inexplicable spike in the correlation
between the Eastern European bond markets and the Latin American bond markets. The same investors who had bought into both markets chose to reduce all

their emerging market bond exposure at the same time.

As you move to smaller markets that are more dependent on non-local investors, the only real way to deal with liquidity risk is to make sure you are highly confident in your view of the market. Then, when short-term imbalances hit, you're prepared to sit them out or build your position even further. Conversely, when the market becomes excessively exuberant, it's a good idea to use the surge in liquidity to cut your exposure, rather than wait for the top of the market. Otherwise, there may not be enough depth in the market to realize fair value.

With these risks in mind, our global risk management strategy utilizes two different but complementary approaches. The first is to make sure that our fund managers use a wide variety of investing styles and strategies. The second is to use extensive modeling to ensure we are monitoring and, if possible, predicting patterns of correlation in the global marketplace. The first strategy is managerial; the second is technological. Both are intended to ensure that our asset allocation gives us the true diversity we believe is the only way to successfully manage the risks of a global portfolio.

MANAGING GLOBAL RISK WITH DIVERSIFIED MANAGEMENT STYLES

We are a small organization of 30 people responsible for a large fund of $14 billion. We manage about a third of that ourselves. Another third is invested in a relatively large number of specialized portfolios. The final third is managed through a somewhat unusual strategic partnership with four investment management firms.

This partnership concept had its genesis six years ago when GTE Investment Management embarked on a program of total quality management, a key theme for our parent company. In addition to the development of strategic partners, it included formal benchmarking activities and process mapping—diagramming absolutely every element and step in the investment process to see how it could be restructured or redesigned to be more efficient and most effective.

We had expected the program to help us manage the investment company better. But the problem we found was more fundamental: the lead we had built on our competitors in terms of long-term performance was shrinking. When we tried to figure out why, we discovered that our asset structure was no longer very different from our peers'. In the late 1980s it had been very different, with a substantial allocation to international assets and a de minimus allocation to real estate—contrary to the conventional wisdom at that time.

Believing as we do that asset allocation is the most important way to produce superior performance, and recognizing that most of our peers now had allocations that looked very similar to ours, we decided that rather than focus on management issues, we should focus on how we allocated our assets. We realized this was a complex problem and we were an organization with limited internal resources. How were we going to solve it? A strategic partnership is one way to gain access to resources you can't afford to own.

We looked for firms with clear expertise in virtually all markets and all asset classes who were willing to enter into a very open relationship, share resources and help us with our research, risk measurement and risk monitoring processes. They had to be willing to designate a champion who could rally the organization's resources for us in bumpy times and were willing to enter into a fee arrangement that would be totally performance driven.

That last requirement, by the way, was something we felt strongly about. One of the reasons we had less emerging market equity exposure than we wanted a few years ago was that the firms managing international equity portfolios for us insisted on creating new emerging markets portfolios with a different fee structure. Our position was that selection of markets was their decision and they shouldn't force us to pay them more to include emerging markets in the mix.

Because our new strategic partnership arrangement was so unusual at that time, we spent a lot of time explaining what we were trying to do to the eight or nine firms we were considering and worked with them as they developed responses to our proposals. We tried to see the partnership from their perspective and anticipate and address any problems they might face, such as the possible compromising of relationships with their other clients. We also outlined the potential advantages for them: considerably more assets to manage, a lot more flexibility and the ability to use their full array of products and skills to demonstrate their value-added. Those key advantages, we argued, would help them market their global asset management and allocation strategies to other large organizations.

Each of our strategic partners has complete freedom to invest in any securities market in the world, within the same risk framework we apply to the overall fund. How do we ensure that this approach produces global diversity—that we aren't giving identical mandates to organizations with essentially the same skill set and strategy? To begin with, we looked for organizations that used different strategies and different methodologies. The organizations we chose ranged in their approach from highly quantitative to highly intuitive. Some are willing to take significant benchmark risk by making very concentrated bets on views they have very, very strong opinions on; others may have just as strong a view, but won't take on as much benchmark risk.

We hold all-day meetings four times a year with all our strategic partners and engage in detailed discussions of how each is doing. These gatherings are quite collegial, but can occasionally have a confrontational undertone. Clearly, these organizations can't help but learn from each other while defending their own approach. Some of that is good, but what we want to avoid is the convergence that comes when people begin to use elements of strategies and methodologies that have worked for others. The question is, will the core approaches remain inherently unique? We're hoping that's the outcome. You can't avoid some small degree of convergence, but we hope it's like a rubber band—you can stretch it just so far and then it reestablishes its own natural form.

We also diversify our global investing style by maintaining a big difference between what we do internally and what we do externally. By policy, our internal portfolio takes a relatively low degree of risk, deviating little from our benchmarks. We won't have stocks in our portfolio that aren't in the benchmark index. That's one of our risk controls. We also have a limit on tracking error, the amount of variability in our portfolio vis-à-vis the benchmark. Although we try to make small bets away from the benchmark and expect a favorable but small value added, we expect our strategic partners to construct much higher-risk portfolios, with higher tracking errors, to achieve their value-added targets.

If someone thought of a way for plan sponsors to contribute company stock while increasing diversification,
they should patent it.

MetLife Diversified
Employer Stock Fund

PATENT PENDING

MetLife®

In our specialized portfolios, on the other hand, we make very concentrated bets, each of which tends to run to several hundred million dollars. We won't make those bets internally because we don't have the expertise. The specialists do and they invest in all kinds of private markets—everything from timberland to private equity in China.

We decide on those niches internally, however; it's one of the prime functions of senior management. We choose specialized managers based on our assessment of both the organization's risk management skill (since we view risk management as an organizational skill) and the individual's investing skill (since we view return value-added as an individual skill, although it generally flows out of the organization's investment process). We also try to find managers who are good at rotational strategies between different styles of equity or categories of assets. That's an area where few managers have had consistent success, but in a shorter time frame it adds diversity to our asset allocation.

Has this approach to managing risk by diversifying management styles succeeded? We will make a formal evaluation at the end of three years, so we're not drawing any major conclusions yet. But so far, the results are a lot better than we'd anticipated. Investment management companies generally promise returns of 100 to 200 basis points above the benchmark but rarely deliver them. We've been realizing returns substantially higher than that.

MANAGE ASSET ALLOCATION TO MINIMIZE CORRELATION

The second thrust of our global risk management strategy is to manage our asset allocation to minimize correlation. Obviously, when we're making asset class decisions, we look at the risks both of the class and the particular implementation of the class. We want a sense of how the class might perform over a very long—say 50-year—time horizon. But for us, one of the essential criteria in the whole exercise is a correlation pattern that's distinctive. Its performance should be independent, or nearly independent, of other designated asset classes. We want to know that we will get true diversification and not just more of something.

Our managers, for instance, use the security markets in the U.S., London and Asia. By their very nature, commodity-based businesses are cyclical assets. What we look for is a cyclical pattern that's earlier or later than the broad economic forces that are driving the overall equity market. That's how you beat the index—by reducing or increasing your exposure to late or early cyclical opportunities. We're looking for independence and stability in different environments, although we recognize that how things correlate in a highly inflationary regime may be different from how they correlate when there's low inflation.

MODELING THE CORRELATION OF GLOBAL MARKETS

To identify how markets and asset classes correlate, we use extensive and detailed global modeling. When we're building or refining a model, which we do regularly, the first thing we do is acquire an economic and financial performance history from our data vendors and use it to analyze long-term economic cycles, or regimes. Correlation of returns isn't a stable relationship, it's regime-dependent. We look carefully at, and try to segment, different regimes that have occurred because at some point we will try to determine what type of regime we're in and anticipate

the likelihood of a transition to another. We want to be able to look at the anticipated patterns of returns in each type of regime.

Our main use of models is to establish what we call a tilt for the quarterly rebalancing of the cash market portfolios that we manage internally. Tilts are the over or underweightings that we choose to make each quarter versus the benchmark. We take a quantitative approach, but we're also believers in gut instinct. We've developed a method to quantify judgment so we can understand and reproduce it—quantifying intuition, if you will. This has gone on for a number of years in the engineering world, where it's called expert systems and we've been working with our strategic partners to apply it to financial market decisions.

We try to anticipate what academics refer to as surprise. In terms of the anticipated performance of securities, a lot of people don't formally consider surprise a factor. It's what you don't expect, so how can you consider it? Yet surprise is indeed a critical factor in determining the risk of a particular exposure.

Every three months, we develop a list of events that may have favorable or unfavorable consequences on a market. If we look at Japanese equities, for instance, we start by talking to economists because they are the people who typically try to take a macro view of what's going on in a country. We ask them about sources of political, economic and market risk, as well as what events might transpire. Will the next election result in a majority government rather than another minority government that's trying to build a coalition? That has a profound impact on the government's latitude to carry out its fiscal policies, so it's an important possibility that economists focus on.

Economists also look for evidence that retail investors are beginning to participate in the Japanese market again. That's another very important issue because, historically, during Japanese equity booms a great deal of the market's liquidity comes from retail investors. Recently, however, there's been a tremendous reduction in the market's liquidity because individual investors are disillusioned over the stock market consequences of the country's political corruption, which has favored large organizations over retail investors.

Economists are usually good at understanding the plate tectonics of the process—what the moving parts are. But they don't seem to do as good a job of getting the timing right. Strategists focus on that issue; they try to determine the relative attractiveness of components in the equity markets, as an example. We massage all the information we've gotten from the economists into a single list and send it to equity market strategists who cover Japan along with two questions: What is the likelihood of these events occurring? And if they do, what would their quantitative effect be on the Japanese equity market? We compile their answers and take them to the portfolio managers who are actually running our Japanese equity portfolio for a reality check. Is this a good map of the events and their likelihood?

MEASURING THE RELATIVE ATTRACTIVENESS OF GLOBAL MARKETS

At the end of the day, we're trying to determine the relative attractiveness of asset exposures throughout the global markets. For instance, if we think that over three years the trend in a particular asset will be in a particular direction, we examine how the trends in all other assets are moving in that period and we look at the relationship of those sets of trends. If we think one of the exposures may be potentially declining, but for political reasons we want to keep a minimum exposure, we ask if we also have assets that are going to have offsetting performance.

We blend together the subjective information, which we have now quantified with other attractiveness measures, to come up with overall attractiveness models. Based on them, we make our judgments. We're trying to produce on average returns about 100 basis points better than a benchmark return.

We believe these macroeconomic factors and various cycles in the market are what give us the chance to anticipate relative over-performance or under-performance in different market sectors. But they are only the beginning of the modeling process. Next, we increase or decrease the amount of concentration in particular portions of the portfolio according to these valuation cycles and macroeconomic factors: what we expect the markets to be doing based on where we are and the rate at which we expect transitions might occur.

SELECTING INDICATORS THAT PREDICT GLOBAL MARKET MOVES

The next step we take establishes policy specifications for a particular strategy. First we define the market we're going to apply the strategy to: with the Japanese equity market, for instance, we define it in terms of the Nikkei 225 index. Then we specify the exposure range a particular strategy is allowed to take, the tracking error it's allowed to have and a number of other very detailed limits to exposures that can be taken, all of which deal with the amount of variation that our portfolios can take at an industry or sector level. This is the risk framework that controls how far any particular strategy can go from a defined neutral position.

Finally, we try to select indicators that help us predict market moves. We've developed three categories of indicators. The first is valuation. We started with a dividend discount model and have a number of indicators that have evolved from

Question:
how can plan sponsors provide diversification using company stock?

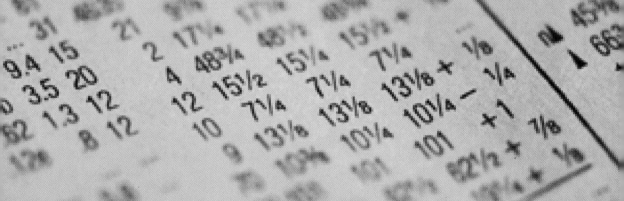

Answer:

MetLife Diversified
Employer Stock Fund

PATENT PENDING

✹ MetLife®

Expect a call from your MetLife Pensions representative.
Can't wait? Visit the MDES Fund website at http://www.metlife.com/mdes or call 1-800-METLIFE.

96091I24(0997)MLIC-LD Metropolitan Life Insurance Company (New York, NY)
The MDES Fund is a group annuity contract separate account.

that. For example, we use an implied discount rate from the dividend discount model based on where analysts expect earnings to go, what the current market price of the security is and our expectations for interest rates.

Next come what we call market liquidity indicators. We use various fixed-income rates to monitor those. We believe that when the real economy is growing it has an increasing need for capital, while in periods of contraction, it's typically giving off capital. To the extent any country's central bank gets ahead of or falls behind the real economy, there is either surplus liquidity or shortfalls in liquidity. Those positive or negative flows are going into or coming out of the financial markets. What we're trying to do is anticipate the degree and direction of those financial market flows based on what the real economy is doing and what the central bank is doing, because when liquidity gets really pumped up, we tend to see rallies and vice versa.

We also use what we call sentiment indicators. These measure short-term imbalances in supply and demand for the securities we're interested in. We believe all securities have some sort of long-term equilibrium value and the short-term value oscillates around that, based typically on aggressive or defensive behavior by market participants. A simple example of this type of indicator is the premium or discount in closed-end mutual funds, like country funds. They trade up and down like equity so the share price is determined separately from the value of the holdings and the difference is an indicator of market sentiment regarding that country.

Most of our indicators are somewhat more complex. We look at all New York Stock Exchange trades on a daily basis and at the specialists' bid-offered price when the trade occurs and determine, according to a set of rules, whether it represents a flow in or out of that security. We would like to do this for non-U.S. markets, too, but the data are not yet available.

A simple example of how we use market sentiment is in emerging markets, which move together in crisis events not because of their fundamentals but because of who the participants are. A very sizable investment by foreign investors moves prices around as shock events occur that are external to those markets. Those undervalued markets can be very attractive and because of our longer time frame, investing in them isn't a risk for us the way it would be for broker-dealer organizations with their limited capital base and more concentrated positions. Their risk is our opportunity. All these indicators are always relating to each other dynamically, depending on how much helpful information we're getting. We have about a dozen of them and we're always looking at new ones.

Once we've chosen our indicators, we construct trading rules based on them. This has two aspects: signals and actions. In simple models we will have three levels of signals: positive, neutral and negative, and corresponding actions of maximum, benchmark and minimum exposures.

We begin testing our indicators through a profitability analysis, both for individual indicators and for groups of them as models. We analyze basic value added, as well as various types of risk and, as a result, we're always changing how we look at risk. We used to look just at volatility, constructing measures like a Sharpe ratio or information ratio. Now we're trying a value-at-risk analysis for some indicators and taking frequent snapshots to see how the value-at-risk is changing. The next step is to look at consistency: how well do the indicators work in different market environments? Finally, we look for patterns—things like the covarients of value added for various combinations of strategies. Do they simply perform well at the same time or are there some differences in how they behave relative to each other? We're always looking for differences in the way markets move, since managing correlation is a key to our global risk management strategy.

TESTING THE MODEL

If all this has gone well, we progress to a broad market test of the model. The first step is an historical test; usually, we go back to January 1960 because that's as early as we can get the level of detail we need. After doing all the statistical studies of hypothetical historical performance and refining the model, we run a paper portfolio as if it were a live portfolio. We'll do that typically for three to six months to detect potential trading problems and to judge its performance. We may refine the model, but we don't usually make major changes. If the model is successful, we'll put in a small amount of money and trade the strategy so it goes through a "curing" period before it's adopted. We go through this process for most all the strategies we manage ourselves, developing some kind of model for almost everything, although—depending on the amount of exposure we have in the area and the amount of information available—some are more complex than others.

We've also gone through this entire procedure to develop option strategies, using the S&P/BARRA Value and Growth contracts and the Morgan Stanley Cyclical and Consumer Growth contracts. While they have a very different construction, they have fairly similar behavior. One object of our research is to try to determine, given their particular posture, how we can develop the most advantageous model with a combination of those contracts, having noted and accepted the biases and efficiencies with which they trade.

The reason we use options is that once we rebalance a cash market portfolio, it stays there for three to four months. But opportunities develop within that period that we'd like to take advantage of. Derivative contracts are an attractive way to do that without disturbing our cash market portfolio. Additionally, our managers operate under incentive fees where they get paid to make judgments on asset classes. We monitor that very closely, but we don't tell them what position to take. That means they may take a position we don't agree with, but we can use our models and access to the derivatives markets to counter it.

About a year and a half ago, we were significantly below our benchmark exposure for Japanese equities because our money managers were collectively bearish. But our models indicated that Japan was extraordinarily attractive. We took a very significant position in equity index options to express our view. In a month or two, the markets started accelerating; when the options expired, our managers were still bearish. We moved half our investment into futures. By the time those expired, our managers were between neutral and slightly bullish and we had realized the value of our contrarian view.

Our strategy—diversifying management styles and strategies and carefully managing the correlation of our asset classes—has not been in place long enough for us to make an absolute judgment on its success. But our returns have increased substantially and we and our managers have been able to out-guess the market often enough to make us believe we're on the right track.

What our experience does teaches us, I believe, is that global risk management is not about avoiding risks, it's about choosing them. We are glad to take size and style bets in the global marketplace, as long as we believe the potential for fair compensation exists.

SMART PILLS

➤ Remember that investing in multiple markets around the world doesn't assure diversity; use a wide variety of investing styles and strategies to achieve that goal.

➤ Consider a strategic partnership as one way to import or use resources you can't afford to own.

➤ Develop a strategy for allocating investment risks, as well as investment funds among your internal portfolios and external managers.

➤ Test and "cure" new investment strategies against current markets as well as against historical data, both on paper and with real money.

CURRENCIES: TO HEDGE OR NOT TO HEDGE?

Richard Rose
Chief Investment Officer
San Diego County Employees Retirement Association

Currency risk has become a major headache for plan sponsors as they attempt to reduce overall portfolio risk through diversification into international securities. It is a problem for which we believe the San Diego County retirement fund[1] has found a solution. We call it our two-armed strategy: we have transformed a currency hedge designed to remove risk into a value-added strategy designed to seek profits—a technique that is replicable by any plan sponsor with more than 5% to 10% of its assets invested in non-U.S. equities.

What began as a simple currency hedge is now considered a separate investment in currencies that has added 242 basis points, annualized, to our return on non-U.S. equity in its first two years of operation. For the two years ending September 1996, the underlying non-U.S. equity return generated by our active managers was 7.79%. The total return after the effects of the currency overlay was 10.21%.

This was not a strategy that San Diego County rushed into. It evolved along with the debate over how to manage the risk of currency exposure, the subject of extended academic debate for the last ten years as institutional investors began to allocate some portion of their assets into non-U.S. equities.

We have not applied this policy to bonds, partly because our non-U.S. fixed-income exposure is so small, but primarily because we do not think it is necessary. Global fixed-income managers have recognized that they are really dealing with two asset classes—bonds and currencies—so they pay much more attention to currency risk and are more capable of dealing with currency exposure than are most equity managers.

A LITTLE BACKGROUND

Ten years ago, global diversification meant equity allocations outside the United States of only about 5% of assets: a very aggressive fund might have invested 10%.

---

[1] The San Diego County retirement fund has a $2.8 billion defined benefit plan with 25% of its assets invested in non-U.S. equity and 4% invested in non-U.S. fixed-income.

At those levels, the amount of currency exposure at the plan level and the technical impact of currency volatility were not of great concern. As international allocations increased and the methods active managers used to deal with currency came under scrutiny, plan sponsors began to pay closer attention.

After examining three to five-year track records for active managers, it became clear that active international equity managers were not paying a tremendous amount of attention to currency risk. They would pick stocks and countries; the plan sponsor was stuck with whatever currency exposure resulted.

Paired with that growing realization was the gradual escalation in the value of the Japanese yen, from around 300 to the dollar starting in the late 1970s, down to 150 to the dollar by the mid-1980s. For a U.S. investor holding yen, this was a big windfall. The currency return was a substantial component of the total return for anyone invested in the Japanese market at this time; that market happened to be soaring, as well.

The average international manager benchmarked to the Morgan Stanley Europe, Asia, Far East Index (EAFE) at the time had significant underweighting to the Japanese stock market and was hurt substantially as the market rose. The result was that managers paid a lot more attention to the foreign exchange issue. Until then, managers interested in currency bets tended to dabble at the margins, and not with a great deal of success. As plans moved toward 15% or 20% exposure to non-U.S. stocks, however, the currency issue became much more important and a debate followed over what to do.

One theory held that the differential in currencies is the market's mechanism for normalizing the differentials in interest rates between countries. Over the long haul, they even out and interest rate parity will result. This theory went on to say that no inherent return is expected from simply owning a currency; any return is really a reflection of differential interest rates. Over the long term, currencies are a zero-sum game.

Since there is a transaction cost to hedging, this argument concluded that a non-U.S. equity portfolio is probably better off being unhedged because in that case it does not incur transaction costs. But whether a portfolio is unhedged or fully hedged really does not make a difference in the end; discrepancies will even out in the long-term. Now, two decades after the yen began to soar from 300 to 115 to the dollar, people are asking, "How long is long?"

A ONE-ARMED STRATEGY

Like many other plan sponsors, we began to question the return our international equity managers were getting. We were paying them to get the country and stock investment right but the currencies were whipsawing their results. International diversification to reduce overall portfolio risk would not succeed if the strategy produced negative returns due to currency fluctuations. Since the impact of currency on returns is easy to measure by directly comparing a portfolio's actual returns to the EAFE benchmark, some plan sponsors, facing the same problem, decided to hedge completely, while other chose to hedge 50% of their portfolios.

We at San Diego County hired a currency specialist to look at the underlying exposures that resulted from the stock and country selections our equity managers were making and selectively remove the currency risk associated with those

Diving into global markets requires understanding risks

The Global Advantage

Fidelity Management Trust Company is dedicated to the global financial services industry. We manage a variety of investment disciplines in both separate and commingled accounts for corporate and public retirement funds, endowments, and foundations. Our 467 investment professionals worldwide, linked by our Global Information Network, give us unparalleled research capabilities.

For information, please contact

Jeffrey Lagarce
Senior Vice President
(617) 563-9444

Fidelity Investments®

investments; for example, to sell yen and buy dollars to selectively hedge away the currency exposure in underlying equities if that was what they considered appropriate in a given situation. This was not a widespread practice at the time, but some other funds also added currency managers as protection in an environment where we had dollar strength and wanted to get out of other currencies.

The problem with the strategy was that all the managers were allowed to do was to remove underlying currency risk. They could look at what the portfolio managers had and, if they didn't like the yen, they could sell yen and buy dollars. The only question was, do we want to own currencies or do we want to own the dollar? It was not a question of do we want to own the yen or the deutschmark. We weren't thinking in those terms yet. These strategies were always a hedge against the dollar.

The dollar was weak throughout the '80s and into the early '90s. In periods of dollar weakness it is better to hold currencies, so the environment did not present these currency managers with a lot of opportunity to add value. If they liked the yen, they couldn't buy more than the hedge required to offset our underlying exposure. It was sort of a one-armed strategy.

THE NEW TWO-ARMED STRATEGY

We analyzed this extended period of dollar weakness and the performance of our currency managers and concluded that our policy was an impediment to success. During this period of dollar weakness, the only action the managers could take was simply to leave the currency exposure that existed. However, we wanted our managers to add value not only in periods of dollar strength, when they could hedge into the dollar, but in periods of dollar weakness, as well.

When San Diego County's retirement fund moved from 15% to 20% international allocation in 1994, we decided to refine the currency overlay program and give our currency managers new responsibilities. We asked them to manage our currency exposure over a three to five-year period in such a way as to add 200 basis points in value to whatever returns the underlying manager was producing.

This is what we call a two-armed strategy. Whereas before they could only remove currency risk that existed in our equity portfolio, with this new strategy they have the opportunity not only to hedge but to actively add value. Although hedging our non-U.S. equity exposure is the basic responsibility, our managers now pursue profits elsewhere, as well. If they like yen and don't like the French franc if we have French franc exposure, they can sell it and buy more yen and they can buy other currencies not in our portfolio. That's what makes this new policy a two-armed strategy: it allows our currency managers to push beyond a simple hedge and add value not only in periods of dollar strength but also in times of dollar weakness.

When we first instituted this policy, our managers immediately added exposure to the yen and were able to take advantage of its move from 100 to about 86 to the dollar. Had they not had that flexibility, they would not have been able to add that incremental value to the yen.

Since then, we have moved into a period of dollar strength, putting the managers back into a situation where the one-armed strategy works and they have hedged out of the yen and into the dollar and added value there, too. Should we go into another period of dollar weakness, they will be able to add additional exposure

"Look Madame Alexandra, I've had it up to here with that "macroeconomic conditions" rant— you of all people should give me a straight prediction on interest rates."

to those currencies they think will outperform other currencies versus the dollar.

We believe in active management. We have identified two active currency managers we have confidence can achieve this mandate. No matter what currencies do, we hope to gain 200 basis points on average above whatever the underlying managers are doing. To my knowledge, no other plan sponsors are using this strategy, although we know that our currency managers, buoyed by their success with our fund, have recommended it to others.

ASSESSING CURRENCY MANAGERS

Currency managers tend to follow two basic management styles. One group is very technically oriented, focusing on short-term trends. These trend followers tend to have very short-term views on currencies—short-term meaning days, weeks, months. The other group studies fundamental macroeconomic conditions and tries to predict how an economy will perform compared to another economy and what the implications are for interest rate differentials. In other words, they try to predict what the implications of currency exchange rates will be, looking out a year or two or three. Some managers borrow from both techniques, so there are different styles to choose from.

San Diego County hired two managers for our retirement fund, one technical and one fundamental. Given that our retirement fund now has $700 million in currency exposure, we felt that was too much for one manager. Hiring two managers with differing approaches was a simple risk control measure.

Our technical manager analyzes where exchange rates have been in the recent past and tries to identify areas where there are resistance points on either the upside or downside. This manager believes currencies will trade in a given range; if he sees a currency outside that range in the short term, he tries to take advantage of the aberration before the currency moves back within its normal range, which he assumes will happen. He may say, in his terminology, that he thinks the yen's a little overdone at this level. If so, he will sell the yen and hope it drops back a little bit.

The fundamental manager studies macroeconomic factors, looking at relative strengths in economies and at the implications for interest rates based on what each economy is doing. Since a lot of what currency exchange rates are about is normalizing differentials in interest rates, if you can get a handle on the direction of relative interest rates, you can adjust your currency positions to capitalize on that over a period of a year or two. This manager tries to capture the longer-term trends in currencies that result from one economy outperforming another or interest rates in one economy declining relative to another economy where interest rates are rising.

Identifying and hiring these managers was not unlike selecting other managers. The process is the same. Currency managers tend to be in specialist firms or in boutiques within larger firms. One difficulty is that not many have been in business for a long time and a plan sponsor needs to have them demonstrate their ability to add value both in periods of dollar strength and in periods of dollar weakness.

One difference in evaluating currency-only managers is that it can be very difficult to make sense of their performance data because the mandates they run for different clients tend to be much more heterogeneous than those of an equity manager who does the same thing for every client. Before you can evaluate their performance, it is necessary to understand what their objectives were, how much flexibility they had with various accounts and what they intended to achieve. There is no really good universe of currency managers for comparison and it is very difficult to compare one manager to another.

Our approach was to examine the performance of individual managers. By performance I mean whether they had the correct view on a currency over a period of time, both in periods of dollar strength and of dollar weakness. The key is their ability to identify trends in currencies and we had to look at that on an individual basis. This is not something we could put on a single sheet of paper, like a scatter chart for an equity manager's risk/return trade-off. We had to understand the mandate of the various accounts we were looking at and see whether the manager had actually been able to pick up currency trends.

It has been particularly interesting to monitor the results of our two currency managers' investment philosophies over the two years that our two-armed strategy has been in place. So far their results have produced a dead heat.

We get a report every day that shows what the currency managers' positions are and how much money each made or lost during the day. Often, I will see that they have completely opposite outlooks and that their exposures basically cancel each other out, although that is usually the case only when nothing in particular is happening and neither of them has a particularly strong conviction. At other times, the two managers may have very similar positions. Sometimes they will have the same general outlook but it will be obvious from the positions they've taken that one has a much stronger conviction than the other about some event or trend.

Achieving financial goals in the Global Market Place can be challenging...

Let Independence be your guide.

- Diversification vs. Other Approaches
- Standard and Customized Benchmarks

Absolute commitment to our institutional clients and their objectives.

Let us tell you more about our international equity management.

To learn more about our products and their unique benefits, please contact Derek Hepworth at (617) 228-8760.

Independence International Associates, Inc.
a subsidary of Independence Investment Associates, Inc.

A VALUE-ADDED STRATEGY

We no longer consider this strategy just a hedge against the currency risk in our equity portfolio. This is now a value-added approach. We believe that adding 240 basis points is proof that our underlying portfolio is also being properly hedged. By adding value, our managers demonstrate that they had us in the right currency, or out of the right currency, at the right time; in other words, they employed active hedging successfully.

Now, instead of worrying about beating this bet or beating this benchmark, we don't have to worry about benchmarks. We just say, we want 200 basis points return on top of what the underlying managers are doing. If the currency managers achieve that goal, they have de facto given us a hedge. If they like the yen but do not have any underlying yen exposure, they would do the same thing—buy yen and sell something else short. In this case, they just have to be mindful of what is underneath.

Our retirement fund has passive exposure to all 20 currencies and 20 countries in the EAFE index, as well as actively managed EAFE exposure. Active managers tend to hold eight or ten, but not all 20. Once a week our custodial bank faxes to our two currency managers a list of the currencies and amounts to which our equity portfolio is exposed and each currency manager is allotted half that exposure. If there is $100 million in yen, for instance, and $50 million in pound sterling, each manager gets $50 million in yen and $25 million in sterling to hedge. If they don't like yen, they can sell it to offset the underlying equity risk and buy other currencies they believe will make money.

In addition, our equity managers are required by contract to report directly to the currency managers any significant currency moves they make intra-week so that our currency risk controls do not get out of sync. The equity managers' benchmark is EAFE unhedged, but our new two-armed policy does not prohibit them from hedging, as well. Their goal is to beat EAFE and occasionally one will have a particularly strong conviction about a currency and will hedge it away. They are using the one-armed strategy, for the most part: if they own Japanese stocks and decide they don't like the yen, they may take the exposure off.

We mark to market daily. We were not satisfied with the accuracy of the daily reports we were getting from our custodian, so we expanded the mandate of a consultant who does the daily mark to market for our managed futures program. Custodians generally do not seem to be attuned to this idea of daily mark to market. They try and they are improving, but we felt it was important to get a daily summary of our positions so that if we see something that does not look right, we can deal with it immediately.

GOING FORWARD

Hedging currencies or investing in currencies as an asset class is admittedly not for every pension plan. A plan with between 5% and 10% of its assets in non-U.S. equities probably need not worry whether to hedge or not to hedge. I do not think it is worth the cost at that level and imbalances will probably work themselves out over time. If something happens to a currency, you won't have to pay dearly for it at the plan level because it is not a big portion of the total fund.

If you view currency as an asset and an area where you can add value, as we do, even if you do not have any non-U.S. exposure, you might want to think about having some exposure to currencies as a value-added strategy. It is not necessary to have any underlying currency risk to hedge in order to make money based on currencies.

The only risk we see in turning a currency hedge into a value-adding asset class is the risk of not making the extra money this strategy has produced for the San Diego County Employees Retirement Association over the last two years—at an annual fee of 18 basis points on the underlying exposure.

There have been fairly significant swings in currencies over the last couple of decades and no matter what strategy a fund employs—not hedging, hedging 50% or 100%—at some point the trend is going to go against whatever strategy you put in place. Our dynamic, two-armed, value-added strategy gives us the best of both worlds because it adds incremental return and, by default, hedges our positions. We believe the benefits of our strategy are clear and will attract more and more adherents as others learn about its success.

 SMART PILLS

- ➤ Review your fund's hedging policy with an eye to turning a profit rather than merely offsetting risk.
- ➤ Consider currencies an asset class that can add value to a global investment strategy.
- ➤ Do not incur the expense of hedging currency exposure if your plan has less than 10% of its assets invested in non-U.S. equities.
- ➤ Remember that a global bond portfolio need not be hedged independently; global fixed-income managers have proven adept at hedging their own currency risks.
- ➤ When conducting a search for currency managers, be aware of the difficulty of assessing performance data fairly due to their extremely varied mandates.
- ➤ Seek managers with sufficient experience who can produce performance data for periods of dollar weakness as well as for periods of dollar strength.

CHAPTER FOUR

THE BENCHMARK DILEMMA: MANAGING THE HIDDEN RISKS

Craig Scholl
Manager, Asset Allocation and Administration
Hewlett-Packard Company

R isk is a concept frequently discussed, generally understood and often misperceived. As investment professionals, our definitions of risk typically differ. Global investors are exposed to political, settlement, valuation and economic risks, as well as several dozen other types of investment-related and operational risks. Because it is unrealistic to address all risks in one chapter, I will focus on some of the challenges inherent in measuring performance relative to a market index when measuring risk and return.

This chapter reviews the appropriateness of standard deviation as a sole measure of risk, discusses alternative measures of return dispersion and provides a framework for understanding the role that various risk measures can have within a plan. Most investors look for the single risk measure that completely expresses a portfolio's return risk. In my experience, there is no one risk number. Moreover, attempts to isolate an individual return risk attribute result in incomplete, if not misleading, analysis. A more complete picture can be developed by grouping desired risk measures into a risk profile that can be standardized appropriately for any individual fund.

Risk profiles for portfolios provide investors with a framework for evaluating and mitigating risks. Each fund should take the time and make the effort required to develop a risk profile that can be commonly applied across portfolios, groups of portfolios and the total fund. This risk profile should include the combination of risk measures that best matches the fund's objectives. For example, a pension plan may focus on funding measures, whereas an endowment could be concerned with meeting spending requirements. A risk that many investors wish to control is the chance of significant deviations from peer performance. By clarifying the fund's core objectives and choosing appropriate risk measures, the investor's true concerns can be addressed. Utilizing a consistent set of measures across portfolios and at the total fund level helps identify the sources of return risks and how they aggregate.

U.S. investors investing outside the United States have a particularly difficult time assessing benchmark return risks due to the lack of extended market history.

The availability of long-term U.S. investment returns allows for a variety of risk assessment techniques that is simply not possible in other markets. Risk measurements made from data based on limited time periods can lead to false or skewed results that may ultimately be misleading.

WHY INDEX RETURNS ARE NOT THE WHOLE STORY

Just as a furniture catalog does not show "fit and finish" details, market index returns cannot provide the sponsor with a complete picture of what to expect from an active portfolio, especially a global portfolio. This is true for two principal reasons: the inclusion of securities not in the index, and security weights within the portfolio that differ from the index weights.

As noted above, investments in securities that are not in the benchmark increase benchmark deviation risk and typically increase expected return. A classic example of this is the "sprinkling" of non-U.S. stocks in a U.S. equity portfolio or emerging markets stocks in an EAFE portfolio. The advantage these non-benchmark securities have is that usually they are low beta investments and can decrease the portfolio's beta. Unfortunately, these may be investments that the sponsor did not intend, or that may duplicate investments in other portions of the plan. Non-benchmark investments must be monitored carefully by the plan sponsor for guideline compliance so that risk and performance drivers for the portfolio are fully understood.

The dispersion of security and security group betas versus the benchmark drives the variability of portfolio alpha within an actively managed universe. For example, the betas of a U.S. large-cap equity index's sectors tend to be closer to one than the betas of a non-U.S. equity index's countries. Therefore, one can expect greater differences in active portfolio alphas from non-U.S. equity mandates than from U.S. equity assignments. This is part of the reason that EAFE's rank in non-U.S. equity universes is much more volatile than the Russell 1000's rank in large-cap U.S. equity universes. Of course, another reason for EAFE's rank volatility is the systematic underweighting of Japan by most managers.

STANDARD DEVIATION

The most common tool used to measure return risk is standard deviation. This measure, while popular, can be misleading if it is used as the sole measure of risk. The interpretation of standard deviation rests upon the assumption that the data is normally distributed. A normal distribution, when graphed, has a bell shape showing most observations around the mean and equally decreasing observations in either direction from the mean. Returns, however, are not normally distributed; data show more observations at the extremes or tails than lie within a normal bell curve distribution. Thus, probability predictions based simply upon standard deviation are best viewed with skepticism.

Standard deviation as a risk measure is best used when accompanied by measures of normality. The most common of these measures are kurtosis and skewness. "Kurtosis characterizes the relative peakedness or flatness of a distribution compared to the normal distribution. Positive kurtosis indicates a relatively peaked distribution. Negative kurtosis indicates a relatively flat distribution. Skewness

"Well, it's clear that your portfolio suffers from a serious case of negative kurtosis."

characterizes the degree of asymmetry of a distribution around its mean. Positive skewness indicates a distribution with an asymmetric tail extending towards more positive values. Negative skewness indicates a distribution with an asymmetric tail extending toward more negative values."[1]

The user of standard deviation can adjust his or her probability expectations by the degree of kurtosis, how closely the distribution of returns fits the normal bell curve. For example, a set of returns where all are very close to the mean indicates a much higher probability of a return that is close to the mean. Conversely, returns that are widely distributed create lower probabilities of returns that are close to the mean. Skewness measures tilts to either side of the mean and is critical in understanding the absolute or relative upside in the return series being analyzed. Both skew and kurtosis can be calculated by any system that measures standard deviation.

OTHER RISK MEASURES

Standard deviation is the risk factor used most commonly by institutional investors. Newer risk measures, such as the information and Sharpe ratios, use standard deviation or a variation of standard deviation as an important component of their risk measurement. Many investors defend standard deviation as the sole measure of risk for reasons of familiarity or convenience. Convenience is important; assuming that returns are normally distributed and uncorrelated over time makes the risk math much more accessible. The use of standard deviation is also defended by proponents of holdings-based risk measures; they say it is measurable and more accurate than returns-based risk calculations. Holdings-based mea-

---

[1] Microsoft Excel on-line help documentation, Version 5.0.

THE FIRST MORGAN

These brass plaques mounted at Morgan Grenfell's headquarters in London symbolize the firm's distinguished history, from its founding in 1838.

Long before J. Pierpont Morgan entered the business, his father Junius established the financial dynasty that was to become the famous House of Morgan. Under Junius' leadership, Morgan Grenfell became the most influential American bank in London.

Today, the Morgan Grenfell Group, a wholly owned subsidiary of Deutsche Bank, is a broad-based international investment management and merchant banking firm with more than 7,000 employees in 50 cities around the world. Through its subsidiaries, the Group manages over $118.5 billion in assets for individual and institutional clients in over 40 countries.

For information about Morgan Grenfell Capital Management, call 212 230-2600.

MG AM MORGAN GRENFELL ASSET MANAGEMENT

sures provide an excellent projection of the current portfolio's future risk, but do not capture the impact of portfolio strategy. There are several investment strategies that have the potential to create non-normal returns. For example, a momentum strategy that uses stop loss rules could create portfolio alphas that are asymmetric.

If standard deviation does not provide a sole measure of risk, what does? The answer lies in the simple truth that there cannot be only one single measure. Just as diversification is the investor's friend in controlling risk, a diversified group of risk measures enhances the investor's assessment of risk. Return risk is best calculated by a thorough review of quantitative indicators. These variability of return indicators include: range analysis, maximum catch-up periods, and upside/downside capture. Hewlett-Packard uses all of these measures when evaluating manager and index performance.

Range analysis, rather than assuming a normal distribution of returns, measures the actual distribution of returns. **Table 1** illustrates the use of range analysis as applied to a review of manager alphas versus a particular benchmark. As you can see, Manager A's alphas have a very wide distribution of values; Manager B's distribution is close to normal; and Manager C's alphas are positively skewed. This is information that would be lost in single measures of risk.

Table 1-Range of Analysis of Monthly Manager Alphas			
		Managers	
	A	B	C
Percentile			
100%	5.11%	2.76%	6.69%
95	2.03%	1.87%	2.04%
75	0.43%	0.60%	0.61%
50	- 0.18%	- 0.16%	- 0.05%
25	- 0.81%	- 1.06%	- 0.78%
5	- 1.92%	- 2.23%	- 1.98%
0	- 5.52%	- 3.55%	- 2.55%
Standard Deviation	1.22	1.22	1.22
Kurtosis	3.90	- 0.10	3.74
Skewness	0.28	- 0.03	0.94

Of universal interest to investors is the length of any period of underperformance. Maximum catch-up asks the question: "If you lose money (on an absolute or relative basis) over a period of time, how long will it take to earn back the money lost?" Using historical data, one can measure the number of periods required to recover from prior below-benchmark returns. The simple case assumes rebalancing. For example, a 20% loss in a portfolio that is rebalanced back to its original value requires a 20% gain to break even. Investors who do not rebalance will have to adjust for the reduced asset base that results from underperformance. In our example a 20% loss now requires a 25% gain to break even.

Upside/downside capture provides a bifurcated view of manager performance versus a benchmark. The question addressed is, "How does portfolio performance compare to benchmark performance in periods of positive and negative index returns?" Portfolio performance is aggregated into two series and typically is stated as a percentage of comparable index performance. **Chart 1** graphs several different portfolios, each with similar returns. This chart illustrates that comparable returns can be obtained from very different paths; it is another way to view

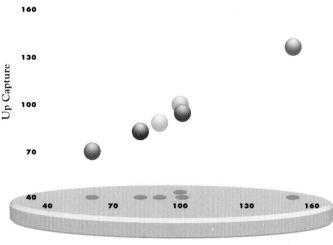

each portfolio's correlation to the benchmark. The portfolios with the lowest correlation are those furthest from a diagonal line that plots where the upside and downside capture ratios are equal. This line goes from the bottom left of the chart through the origin to the top right corner.

MANAGER GUIDELINES

After a tree fell on my house, my wife and I knew what we needed to do. Finding the perfect contractor and developing a sense of trust in his work was only the first step. We still needed a contract that clearly established what work would be done and when payments would be made. Manager guidelines serve as the plan sponsor's risk preference contract. A critical step is to create guidelines that accurately describe the portfolio's investment boundaries. The sponsor's goal should be to include all of the investments that make that manager right for the fund's assets, while precluding securities and strategies that have not been reviewed by the sponsor.

For guidelines to work, both parties must understand the investment parameters and the process for verifying compliance. The verification discussion should include a review of tolerance levels and periodicity. Tolerance levels should specify the degree of accuracy. For example, if a 10% limit exists, is 10.1% acceptable? Timing options include the portfolio's always being in compliance, when trades are made or at particular frequencies (monthly, quarterly, etc.).

The key issues for portfolio guideline agreements include the benchmark, permitted securities, and exposure limits or diversification requirements. Benchmark specifications help communicate the sponsor's return expectation and risk preferences. The creation of a clear and comprehensive listing of permitted securities should eliminate any ambiguity or misunderstanding. The security list can refer to securities by asset class, country of origin, credit rating, currency or any of a long list of criteria. Diversification criteria serve as the core of most guideline documents and provide protection against dramatic differences between the index and portfolio returns. The best diversification guidelines address all key sector exposures and create measurable boundaries.

A portfolio's benchmark provides the cornerstone of the plan sponsor's expectations. The benchmark may be a single index, a combination of indices or a normal portfolio. In some cases the sponsor may choose a combination of benchmarks, against each of which the portfolio will be measured. For example, a portfolio may have a market index benchmark and an absolute return expectation. How a portfolio is measured against the benchmark is also important. The following questions must be answered: What is the measurement time period? What is the expected relative performance? What level of tracking error (relative performance variation) is expected? What will be the source or calculation agent of benchmark returns?

One caveat regarding multi-country portfolio benchmarks: most non-U.S. and global universes show the benchmark index varying significantly in rank across periods. As discussed earlier, this is due in part to the dispersion of country returns and systematic underweighting of countries that form a large portion of the index.

Sponsors may wish to consider alternative weighting schemes. A capitalization-weighted index makes a great deal of sense when there is a free flow of capital from one sector of the index to another, insuring reasonable relative valuation levels. This free flow of capital exists within an asset class in a single country. Between asset classes, even within a country, investor segmentation and transaction costs restrict capital flow. Between countries there are many impediments to the free flow of capital; the valuation of most markets is driven by local investors. Given the circumstances, multi-country investors may find that non-capitalization-based indices meet their needs best.

In addition to risk parameters, the guidelines should specify verification and notification processes. Each asset class will have issues specific to that particular strategy but, by adopting a common set of principles, the sponsor will assure itself of guidelines that keep the portfolio out of unintended investments while providing the manager with the room to create the best returns possible.

Guidelines are only as good as they are current. Review yours with your managers and investment committee on a regular basis to insure against surprises.

The well-informed plan sponsor matches his or her fund objectives to a risk profile applied to the total fund, asset classes and individual portfolios. Ongoing qualitative reviews of risk exposures increase the knowledge applied to portfolio allocations and help dispel the "black box" nature of many risk assessments. Guidelines serve as the core of any risk management program and are a necessary prerequisite for the successful management of any plan.

SMART PILLS

➤ Express return risk in multi-measure risk profiles.

➤ Understand that global investors using only standard deviation have an incomplete view of investment risk.

➤ Use standard deviation along with tests measuring how well the return distribution fits the normal curve.

➤ Include measures that do not assume normal distributions to complete risk profiles. These measures include range analysis, maximum catch-up and upside/downside capture.

➤ Design risk profiles to meet your fund's own definition of risk.

➤ Recognize that risk profiles are not an end in themselves; they provide a basis for discussion and risk management implementation with portfolio managers.

➤ Develop clear and comprehensive portfolio investment guidelines to prevent problems. Update them regularly.

We're Not Afraid of Commitment

In fact, at John Hancock Funds we've built our business on a firm commitment to helping our *institutional clients* succeed. ■ Institutional investors have trusted John Hancock Funds to manage their assets since 1968. That's because we earn their trust each day through our expertise in domestic and overseas fixed income and equity markets, by adhering to clearly defined investment strategies and by exceeding our clients' expectations for quality and service.

At the heart of our approach to institutional investment management are the principles upon which our organization was founded:

■ *Total team approach to portfolio management and research* — Each portfolio is the result of the team's best ideas.

■ *Disciplined investment process* — Every decision we make is within the context of a clear strategy and our clients' objectives.

■ *Focused fundamental research* — Independent fundamental analysis and in-depth evaluations are central to our ability to achieve proven results for our clients.

For more information on our institutional investment management commitment, please contact James V. Bowhers, Executive Vice President, at (617) 375-4880.

JOHN HANCOCK FUNDS
A Global Investment Management Firm

John Hancock Funds, Inc. 101 Huntington Ave., Boston MA 02199

INTRODUCTION

As the following Roundtable discussion clearly demonstrates, global risk measurement is an area where one size does not fit all. John Lawson's needs in running the single, public plan of the Police Department of Houston are very different from those of Desmond Mac Intyre, who monitors risk for multiple corporate plans at General Motors Investment Management Corporation. The liquidity requirements and liability structure faced by Larry Siegel at the Ford Foundation differ from those Robert Spooner considers when he models how various market conditions can affect Eastman Kodak.

Despite that caveat, however, there are some commonalities to their four approaches to risk measurement and risk management. Perhaps the most important is that they have all thought seriously about which risks are most important to their individual funds and have put into place systems to monitor those specific risks. Secondly, there are huge elements of common sense and logic in all their approaches.

For example, Mr. Lawson boils risk down to what may be the most fundamental issue for a pension plan: the ability to pay benefits when due. He focuses on asset allocation as a major input into the Houston Police fund's ability to do just that. He then asks, "What if the return assumptions from that asset allocation are wrong? Will the plan have enough assets to pay liabilities?" In risk jargon, he has identified the "model" risk inherent in his asset allocation model, identified "market" risk as relevant, done a shortfall probability analysis and factored in liquidity and liability structure.

Introductions should not summarize the following chapter and this one won't. It is worth noting, however, that in a few short pages these four plan sponsors identify scores of risks. Mr. Siegel identifies market risk as the most important to the Ford Foundation, given the structure of its portfolio. Mr. Spooner cites performance-related risks. He also adds a risk that many plan sponsors share, but few make explicit: the risk of "embarrassing the corporate plan sponsor through negative publicity..." Mr. Mac Intyre views "risk in a holistic sense" and cites ten risk categories. Moreover, the risks keep changing. As Mr. Lawson says, "Anytime a financial organization says we're done, it's asking for surprises."

What emerges then is a massive, perhaps indeterminable, list of ways things can go wrong. Even worse, the list is then compounded by the unfortunate reality that new mistakes keep getting made, lengthening the list further. Faced with such a daunting prospect, some institutional investors may be tempted to throw up their hands. At the very least, it's hard to know where to begin.

That is precisely why eleven plan sponsors came together to create a set of model risk standards for institutional investors and institutional money managers.[1] Think of the standards as the road map outlining a set of questions that help you identify and measure the risks which matter to your fund. The standards then offer a set of suggestions to help you measure and manage your risks. In effect, they provide a toolbox full of current risk measurement and risk management tools. The standards don't dictate which tool you should use on a particular problem, but they do provide a sufficient set of hammers, screwdrivers and wrenches from which you can choose.

In the end, remember that your fund is unique. What is appropriate for Eastman Kodak may be overkill for you or may not deal with all your issues. As Mr. Spooner said in talking about value-at-risk as a quantitative tool, "Judgment is necessary!"

Enjoy rummaging through the toolbox provided by both this Global Risk Roundtable discussion and the new risk standards.

Jon Lukomnik
Deputy Comptroller for Pensions
City of New York
Office of the Comptroller
Member, Risk Standards Working Group

---

[1] A complete list of "The Risk Standards for Institutional Investment Managers and Institutional Investors" may be accessed through the World Wide Web at www.cmra.com.

This detail from an 1878 Atlanta Mining Company stock certificate features Atlas. In Greek mythology Atlas was condemned by Zeus to forever bear heaven and earth on his shoulders.

HUNDREDS OF EMPLOYEES,

EACH WITH A DIFFERENT NEED.

WE KNOW HOW THE AVERAGE

BENEFIT MANAGER FEELS.

Overseeing your employees' futures can be overwhelming. • But the right partner can help you choose the right investment products at the right time. For example, our Institutional Trust Services offer a broad fund selection, including selective strategic fund alliances. Working together, we'll help you bundle retirement benefits like 401(k), IRA rollovers and financial planning. Or set up non-qualified plans for highly compensated employees who need to invest more than a traditional 401(k) allows. Together we'll continue to assess your employees' needs so that you'll be able to meet them. • Which can take a huge weight off your shoulders. To find out more, call 1-800-917-9343.

GLOBAL RISK ROUNDTABLE
MEASURING AND MANAGING GLOBAL RISKS:
INNOVATIVE SOLUTIONS TO MEET DIFFERENT NEEDS

E very pension plan manages risk in different ways depending on its size, resources and objectives. Increasingly, the techniques used to measure and control investment risk overseas are the same as those applied domestically, thanks in large part to the increasing capabilities and responsibilities of custodian banks. The very different approaches and tools these four innovative plan sponsors use to measure and control the various risks they deem most important offer informative and useful ideas that can be implemented by plan sponsors of any size.

PARTICIPANTS IN THE ROUNDTABLE DISCUSSION

John Lawson,
Executive Director
**Police Department of
Houston Pension System**
$1.4 billion in assets
Currently being restructured
with new targets:
   25% international equities
   13% global fixed-income

Laurence B. Siegel,
Director of Quantitative Analysis
The Ford Foundation
$8.4 billion assets:
   13.5% international equities
   7.2% international bonds

Desmond Mac Intyre,
Director of Risk Management
**General Motors
Investment Management
Corporation**
$65 billion Defined
Benefit plan assets:
   20% non-U.S. investments

Robert D. Spooner, Ph.D.,
Manager Pension Investments
Eastman Kodak Co.
$8 billion assets:
   20% non-U.S. stocks
   4% non-U.S. fixed-income
   3% non-U.S. private
     investments

Q. WHAT RISKS MATTER MOST TO YOU?

Lawson:

The number one risk that concerns me is whether or not we will be able to pay benefits to our membership whenever they are due.

Once we recognize that risk and determine what our liability streams are, the question is how to structure a portfolio of investments so that we can meet those demands. And that gets into the asset allocation process. The risk in the asset allocation process is whether or not our projections of the future, or input to whatever optimization process is utilized, are accurate.

Let's assume that our view of the future is reasonable and we look at absolute risk. Our asset allocation says we should be able to return 10% over time and our actuary says we need 8% in order to pay benefits. If we think we're going to make 10% and know that we might make as low as 6% or as high as 12% to 13%, we have to ask ourselves, "Is that expected risk and the risk we have to take to make that expected return worthwhile?" If everything goes exactly wrong and we miss that target, what happens to the pension plan over a long period of time? Do we have the assets to make up the benefits?

Most of us, especially pension plan trustees, view investments from the 1980s forward. Everyone seems to have conveniently forgotten the late '60s and the '70s when everything did go exactly wrong. If there was a turn to be made, it was always down. Can our plan absorb not meeting that target over an extended period of time—and how long can it afford to do so?

On the international side, we use the EAFE index as a benchmark, but we have found that our managers all avoid Japan, which is 30% to 40% of EAFE. So all of a sudden there's a big hole there. We chose to address that by hiring a manager with a Japan-only mandate to fill the void. That's fine until we wake up and find Japan is down 5% or 11%. That begins to test our intestinal fortitude to stick to our guns—which is another risk. People tend to give up just about the time things turn around and change; we must have commitment and perseverance over a long period of time to believe that our asset allocation will take us where we want to go from an actuarial standpoint.

Mac Intyre:

We look at risk in a holistic sense right across the organization. To help us do this we have recently developed standards of best practice for ten risk categories: compliance, corporate/financial, credit/counterparty, fiduciary, liquidity, market, modeling, operational, monitoring and systems. The standards are similar to those produced by the Risk Standards Working Group, and while they largely reflect other industry-wide efforts, we fine tuned them to meet our own unique organizational and cultural needs. It is worth saying that, while they touch upon the headline risks we are all too familiar with, they are in all honesty more mundane in nature. One has to get the foundations right first.

However, like John Lawson, I believe the biggest determinant of risk is in the asset liability modeling process we go through every three years. That process sets the long-term asset allocation policy and range of assets we invest in and it is essential that we understand exactly what we are buying into.

For me, the job of risk management is to understand the policy one has bought into and make sure that once we've identified the critical path, we stay on it. It is important to reaffirm one's investment policy on a regular basis as well as the assumptions underpinning one's analysis.

In day-to-day terms, monitoring risk is probably one of the most obvious risks we face. This means dealing with the potential for losses due to a breakdown in due diligence, which is inherently a multidimensional problem facing us at the security level, the individual manager level and the overall plan level. It is very time intensive to monitor, especially with the size of our asset base and the number of mandates we cover. Monitoring risk includes manager relations; the impact of investment initiatives that were not fully understood at the outset and the potential of unintended consequences; and the monetary impact on the portfolio and the fund itself if managers violate guidelines, engage in unauthorized transactions, excessive concentrations and so on.

Siegel:

Because the Ford Foundation has a large, diversified portfolio that does not use leverage or short selling or any derivative strategies other than currency hedging, the most important risk for us is the fluctuation of markets. The risk of having performance very different from the markets is less important because we tend to stay fully invested and have broadly diversified positions.

Spooner:

There are several risks I consider most important for our plan to manage: absolute loss of capital, especially from an event-related loss; underperformance compared to our benchmarks; actuarial risk that falling interest rates might result in underfunding our liabilities; and improper manager practices that could result in investment underperformance.

These risks are not unique to domestic or global investments; they apply to the pension fund as a whole. I think the improved diversification that comes from investing in the best opportunities around the globe reduces risk, especially if proper monitoring and control measures are implemented.

Q. How Do You Measure These Risks?

Lawson:

We do believe in alpha, that there are managers who have the ability to achieve returns above the benchmark. This idea leads to residual risk—the standard deviation of that excess return above the benchmark. One must look at these bands through time to see whether you're rewarded or punished for having active managers. Can they, in fact, return what you think they can and repeat their historical track record?

In a perfect world, we would purchase some of the tools available now. Unfortunately, a plan the size of the Houston Police Department does not have the budget to be able to afford those very, very expensive products. We do have some tools in house. Also, we're on line with our master custodian and we can get some analytics through them. We have access to comparative data and if we want to see where our bets are, relative to a particular benchmark, we can certainly do that.

How do I get Value at Risk measures without spending a fortune?

If you're looking to implement Value at Risk measures for an investment portfolio, but don't want to add staff or install extensive software, consider the RAROC 2020^{SM} solution. RAROC 2020 has leading portfolio-wide analytics available and you can outsource Value at Risk reporting to the experts in the RAROC 2020 service bureau. Institutional investors have found this a cost-effective route to getting superior risk information, especially formatted with an investor's needs in mind.

While other systems report your aggregate level of risk, RAROC 2020 also pinpoints its exact location. Instead of flooding you with raw data, RAROC 2020 presents you with comprehensive, yet accessible and useable reports.

In a world where new financial products are developed daily, not having precise risk analysis tools could lead to missed opportunities, intolerable risks, or perhaps both.

Call Michelle McCarthy at (206) 325-2020 to learn more about RAROC 2020. A meeting with us will help clarify whether outsourcing is for you.

Bankers Trust

Architects of Value

We can determine where we stand and where our decisions are taking us and we do so on a continual basis. I have a CFA on staff and one of his mandates is to monitor these situations, so he's in there daily, evaluating the different managers to see what's going on. We review trades on a trade-by-trade basis and evaluate how they relate to the portfolio mandate.

For instance, a couple of years ago, I pulled up the previous day's trades of a growth manager with a mandate for long-term growth and found he had bought a small-cap stock. A couple of days later, I saw that he'd flipped out of it and for that two-day exposure, we made $200 after expenses. I checked the wires to see if there was anything to explain the transaction, then called the manager. His explanation basically told me that he was paying the broker.

This brings up another risk. Even if you hire someone and give them a mandate and discretion to run a portfolio, from a fiduciary standpoint you can't just walk away from it. There must be some structured oversight that allows us to monitor our benchmark-relative positions.

Mac Intyre:

In meeting our return and funding requirements, we stress-test our asset liability results and review our capital market assumptions on an annual basis. Assuming we've got that right, our next job is to make sure we are investing in line with our benchmark, staying on the critical path. In other words, are we within the minimum and maximum investment targets for each asset class?

GMIMCo has an asset mix system that allows us to monitor our benchmark-relative positions using both a bottom-up and a mandated approach. However, this is a costly and cumbersome exercise because we have three custodians and a broad mixture of investments that have to be priced.

At the asset class level, we have individual business units in control; they are benchmarked against set targets and are led by one of our managing directors. Thus, there is accountability—the greatest form of risk control. Each asset class has an identified alpha target and we select managers using an optimization approach to achieve this target.

We measure the performance of all our portfolios against agreed-upon benchmarks tailored to individual styles and return targets. Performance, in the main, is measured monthly, using a rolling three-year investment horizon. These figures are qualified with reference to other like managers, their tracking error, semi-variance, standard deviation, stock characteristics, style, etc. One useful measure we use is the information ratio, the unit of return for every unit of risk taken on. Thus, we endeavor to risk-adjust the performance of our managers. For fixed-income, we would obviously employ measures such as duration. We also have external performance measurement supplied on a quarterly basis.

We believe it's important to profile our managers to ensure that they are generating their returns in line with their investment process, otherwise a good quarter could be due just to random luck. In this way, performance attribution is a very good risk control. To cover the broader issues, we meet with our investment managers at least twice a year for full face-to-face reviews.

For our derivatives, which are all exchange-traded except FX, we employ value-at-risk, VAR. The important thing to note here is that for GMIMCo, derivatives are a means of risk control, typically used for hedging purposes, and thus, they should not be monitored in isolation. VAR is used mostly to determine our cash cover needs, but ever so cautiously, and it is subject to extreme stress-testing.

Securities lending is another area worth mentioning. The concern for us here centers on the investment risk of the collateral provided, as we have full indemnification of our collateral. You have to be careful to ensure that you're benchmarking the investment of this collateral first, and second, monitoring the potential mismatch between the maturity of stocks on loan versus the underlying collateral. Some form of GAP analysis or duration analysis is warranted here. We are even considering VAR analysis for this task.

Siegel:

We measure our risk statistically, using beta, duration, tracking error, currency risk and total risk. These measures are calculated for each portfolio and for various aggregations, such as all domestic equities and all international equities, every quarter using a five-year data window.

Because we use five years of data, a change in the risk profile of a portfolio, even a dramatic change, will not show up very quickly. There are faster ways to do it, but they would take a greater commitment to quantitative analysis. An approach that responds more quickly to changes in risk is cross-sectional analysis, which takes a "snapshot" of portfolio characteristics at a point in time, rather than taking an average over time. We don't use cross-sectional analysis because it is very labor-intensive and may have high out-of-pocket costs.

Our custodian provides daily data feeds so that we can see our holdings every night. We take comfort in the fact that the information is available, even if we don't look at it every day. It is fed to our desktops so when we need the information, it is there.

There are other risks which fall more into the category of unintended risk— that is, risks we may be exposed to without knowing it: counterparty risk, fraud, theft risk, derivative disasters. Even if we don't have any derivatives, one of our managers could be an operating unit of a company that experiences disaster and we could be endangered that way. We chose our custodian, a large U.S. bank with an operating subsidiary in London, to minimize these unintended risks. Some assets, such as private equity, cannot be custodied this way, but it's not possible to guard against everything.

Spooner:

In addition to monitoring each manager's portfolio holdings, we use several different quantitative tools to help measure and adjust our portfolio's expected future return and risk exposure. For our strategic planning horizon of three to five years, we apply modern portfolio theory models to create an efficient frontier—that is, the portfolio mix of asset classes which maximizes the expected rate of return for each level of portfolio risk. We update our projected return, correlation and volatility assumptions annually to assure they reflect our staff's current thinking. This is most useful for measuring the risk of underperformance versus benchmarks.

I think that most of the benefit from this effort actually comes from the staff's discussing the reasoning behind their expectations for future returns, risks and correlations for different asset classes. When we've completed the exercise, we collectively understand the rationale supporting the actions we want to take. The formal outcome of this exercise, a written summary of assumptions and asset allocation targets, simply documents our collective thinking.

I'd offer the cautionary comment that modern portfolio theory may understate risk because it assumes prospective returns are normally distributed when, in fact, return distributions typically have "fat tails". Fat tailed distributions mean that the probability of adverse results is actually higher than might otherwise be expected. Intuitively, a higher than normal probability for extreme negative outcomes is the result of unusual or unpredictable events—an oil embargo, war in Bosnia, etc. The only way I know to control and manage these risks is through extensive portfolio diversification.

To improve operational monitoring of risk, we have explored value-at-risk techniques. VAR attempts to estimate the probability of near-term loss or gain by analyzing the actual securities in a portfolio given certain assumptions about economic and financial factors like inflation, interest rate or exchange rate changes. VAR is most useful for measuring the risk of absolute loss of capital, or the risk of missing a benchmark level of performance—near term.

We have found VAR to be very data intensive. We were able to model about 80% of our public securities and we did not attempt to model our illiquid, private investments. As yet, we have not found VAR's benefits to be worth the cost. However, I believe that VAR analysis will become more widely available in the years ahead, perhaps through custodians who can benefit from economies of scale to lower the cost.

About three years ago, we used simulation forecasting models to analyze the likely future funding requirements of our plan sponsor. With simulations, we were able to determine how our funding requirements might vary for different portfolio asset mixes and interest rate environments. I would recommend an update of this analysis about every five years unless significant changes occur in the pension fund's portfolio or in the interest rate outlook.

Finally, monitoring of third-party manager practices required extensive upfront due diligence, followed by continuous monitoring by the plan sponsor's staff.

Q. How Do You Check The Accuracy Of Your Risk Measurements?

Lawson:

We observe trades daily. We also require that each of our managers gives us a report on a monthly basis that describes everything that was sold, everything that was purchased and the reasons why. Of course, what we're trying to assure and keep focused in our minds is why we hired each manager. What slot in our structure, in our asset allocation, are they filling? And we're trying to keep the managers focused on the same thing.

Mac Intyre:

We take the "full belt and braces" approach. Every single transaction is audited by an independent third party, which is a huge risk control. I believe up to 40 people are employed by our consultant to service our account alone. They look for everything from uncaptured dividends to rights issues, etc. Often the differences are a

By joining forces with GAT we opened more than a few new Windows.™

BARRA is proud to announce the availability of Windows-based software to cover all your fixed income analytical needs.

It just goes to show you, three companies are better than one. In merging with RogersCasey and Global Advanced Technology Corp. (GAT), we've increased our ability to meet your risk management needs with a complementary suite of capabilities, products and consulting.

Now fixed income professionals can enjoy Cosmos-U.S., our new Windows-based portfolio risk management software, along with Decision, the next generation Windows platform for fixed income security analysis. All backed by leading-edge research and support worldwide.

In working as one, we can give you more insight into all aspects of portfolio management than ever before. All from a single source. No matter what your asset class, user environment or office location.

To find out more about our new capabilities, please call **1-510-548-5442** *or visit us online at* **www.barra.com.**

ⓢ **BARRA**

R O G E R S C A S E Y
A MEMBER OF THE **BARRA** GROUP

G Λ T

1-510-548-5442   www.barra.com

matter of definition, but real errors do occur. When you're managing investments for nine individual pension plans as we are, it's very important to assure that we are allocating all of the income flows properly. Everyone has to get his or her slice of the cake.

We also have independent performance measurement supplied to us on a quarterly basis. Thus, performance measurement is subject to a three-way check using our internally generated figures, the managers' figures and those of the third-party performance measurement company. These figures are reviewed by senior management on a regular basis, so any problem areas are highlighted early. No one likes surprises.

It is unrealistic to believe that one can check each line investment in an unautomated environment. For this reason, we have been pushing our custodians to provide exception reporting on all of our mandates versus their investment guidelines. This is something new. Currently, we have three custodians helping us. I think this is probably a very important development for the whole industry.

I don't believe in totally event-driven exception reporting, such that you can follow it on an hour-by-hour basis or even on a daily basis. If you can't trust your managers to that degree, you should terminate them. I think exception reporting on a monthly basis is generally sufficient. It has to be done on an exception basis because too much data, too much paperwork will not be reviewed and it's fundamental that exception reports are acted upon when they occur.

One of the other major things we're doing in terms of risk management is demanding audited reports from our external managers with specific reference to their operational controls in line with the latest Statement on Auditing Standards (SAS). It's possible going forward that we will provide them with a set of standards like those of the Risk Standards Working Group—and get their auditors to sign off that they are in compliance with them. It's important to remember that a lot of the problems experienced in the industry to date were due to poor management and controls. Performance is not always the best indicator of trouble to come. Constant attention is necessary to ensure that things are going according to plan.

At the organizational level, we employ a matrix structure that provides for a degree of overlap between areas. This creates an open environment for discussion and, indeed, risk control. We have very clear separation of duties between our investment areas and our back office. Everybody is encouraged to question; everybody is a risk manager.

Siegel:

The most revealing single exercise that we can do is simply to compare manager returns with market returns to see if our managers are taking more or less risk than the market. It can also tell us the flavor of the difference. The difference may be basically random, caused by holding a small number of stocks in a large stock market, or it may be thematic—the manager is betting on interest rates, currencies or some other systematic factor.

At present, we're looking at the returns of a persistently under-performing manager, a global asset allocator, and trying to figure out whether the manager has experienced a deterioration of skill in his craft or if his style has simply gone out of favor. This is a very tricky analytical challenge because the return data would look the same in either case. To solve this problem, we need to look at the returns of other managers with a similar style to see if our manager has experienced unusually low returns relative to his peer group. If so, the skill level has probably deteriorated.

Spooner:

All the quantitative and qualitative tools have shortcomings that limit their accuracy in measuring risk. For instance, variables are rarely normally distributed, but most quantitative tools assume the rates of return are normally distributed. The only certainty is that some unforeseen event will occur, have an impact in the marketplace and, therefore, affect investment results, sometimes positively and sometimes negatively. Diversification into many different asset classes and investment strategies, as uncorrelated with each other as possible, provides more comfort than trying to measure risk more accurately.

Active monitoring and control procedures, rather than measurement procedures, are more appropriate for some categories of risk—the risks of investment manager non-compliance with guidelines, for instance. Our procedures require in-depth due diligence before hiring a manager and then continuous follow-up monitoring by our staff and custodian, often by using computerized monitoring algorithms. For instance, working with our custodian we have implemented monitoring algorithms designed to verify that each investment manager remains in compliance with his guidelines. This has been particularly useful for monitoring daily compliance with guidelines for the use of derivatives.

Q. WHICH RISKS SHOULD BE MANAGED AT THE FUND LEVEL AND WHICH BY INVESTMENT MANAGERS?

Lawson:

At the portfolio level, managers should have discretion within their described mandate. They should be able to manage all the risks involved so long as it's within the mandate. If we hire a small-cap manager and find that he's trading only in large-cap stocks like GE, the pension fund suffers because our asset allocation becomes useless. This assumes that we have the allocation right in the first place.

From the fund's standpoint, we manage risk in relation to the asset allocation and structure. And then we manage risk from a fiduciary standpoint by providing in-depth oversight of our managers.

Mac Intyre:

I certainly think that at the aggregate asset class level and at the plan level, the composite of risk for our investments is solely our responsibility. However, we cannot abdicate our responsibility for understanding the sources of return and risk at the portfolio level. We need to work with our managers to ensure that they produce our required analytics and that we get independent verification. This often proves to be a symbiotic process: we both learn from each other, especially when it comes to new products or areas of investment. While the portfolio manager is responsible for the risk management of his portfolio, we have to ensure that the risk being taken is consistent with our expectations.

Siegel:

Our outside managers manage the money we give them, we measure the returns and the risk. We don't manage the risk. Managing the risk implies decision-making authority over the portfolio such that when there's a risk you don't want to take, you don't take it. If we believe a manager is acting inappropriately, they'll hear about it. But they have complete discretionary authority within the written guidelines.

We've sometimes been surprised and disappointed by the extent to which otherwise sophisticated managers have poor risk measurement, return attribution and quantitative skills. Sometimes they can make high returns in the market without knowing how they did it. Even the first level of attribution of an international portfolio—return to country selection, currency selection and stock selection—is sometimes not available from the manager and a consultant has to be hired to calculate those numbers. Most of our domestic assets are managed internally so the director of equity investing can access whatever tools he wants.

Spooner:

I believe absolute and relative performance risks and actuarial funding risk need to be managed and therefore measured at the fund level. We focus on building a globally diversified portfolio geared to achieving the highest expected future returns within the risk parameters that our investment committee has determined to be prudent.

Both plan sponsors and investment managers are responsible for implementing operational controls. The plan sponsor needs to perform proper due diligence and implement good monitoring procedures to ensure that assets are being managed properly. But this must be done in a manner that does not restrict managers from producing the best possible results. In turn, investment managers must also implement measurement and control procedures to ensure that assets under their control are invested in a prudent manner, consistent with the investment guidelines. It is especially important that investment managers implement stringent internal control procedures to prevent inadvertent guideline violations or "rogue trader" losses.

Q. How Do You Manage Investment Managers Around The World?

Lawson:

In the electronic age, managers are a mere phone call or e-mail away. We have the same oversight over our overseas managers that we have domestically because our custodian has those capabilities. It is all part of the same oversight function. The same processes are used for each mandate in the portfolio, whether it's domestic fixed-income, global fixed-income or alternative investments.

Mac Intyre:

About 20% of our assets are international in nature; however, not all of these are run by non-U.S. firms. Interestingly, there has been an increasing trend toward hiring U.S. managers to run international mandates because they are generally

Different.

HOLL INTERNATIONAL LLC
International Money Management

more sophisticated in terms of having a clearly defined investment process and good risk and performance analytics. However, it's important to say that we treat all investment managers the same whether they are in the U.S. or Europe. We demand the same high standards from all of them and to help us manage them we have a dedicated investment group that deals solely with international investments.

Communication, generally, is not a problem. Data is fed in the normal way to our custodians on a daily basis no matter where the managers are in the world. Frequent on-site visits are the norm, as is teleconferencing, e-mail, etc.

Spooner:

As part of the hiring process, we conduct on-site visits, reference checks and ask the manager to complete a detailed questionnaire in order to develop baseline information on his organization and performance record. Once a manager is hired, our custodian's monthly reports detail each account's securities holdings and recent trading activity. When appropriate, and certainly whenever derivatives are used by the manager, we have the custodian computerize a daily scan of the manager's portfolio to ensure compliance with guidelines.

In addition, we recently set up limited liability trusts for each separate account where the manager is authorized to use derivatives. These trusts ensure that a manager cannot expose our plan to losses in excess of the account's underlying net asset value. In effect, this gives our separate accounts the same limited liability protection that a commingled fund or partnership offers. We instituted these trusts last year and so far have created 14 of them. Our custodian is able to track these as individual entities and consolidate them for oversight purposes.

The biggest challenge was to develop a legal structure that would create true, independently operating trusts by formalizing all transactions that occur among the different trusts. For example, we now have contracts between the trusts for securities lending and cash management activities.

Even though creating the limited liability trusts required considerable effort, their ongoing maintenance costs are minimal. The trusts were deemed to be the least expensive, but a very effective, way to allow the staff to have total fund oversight while still controlling the downside risks of certain investment strategies which use derivatives.

Q. DO YOU ADJUST RETURNS FOR RISK AND IF SO, HOW?

Lawson:

No, we do not. We believe that the major advantage of asset allocation is the diversification of risk. In fact, our structure requires some managers to have higher tracking errors to the underlying index. This is by design. However, the portfolio is put together so that the overall risk is acceptable with the level of return, given our liability structure.

Mac Intyre:

As I indicated earlier, we monitor a manager's performance in relation to a given benchmark and compare the risk characteristics of a portfolio against its benchmark. We get a more complete picture by monitoring a manager's standard deviation, tracking error, the beta of the portfolio and his downside risk. Ultimately, we aim to measure a manager's information ratio—the unit of return for every unit of risk in the portfolio. A manager may be beating his benchmark but, if he's taking excessive risk, it will show up.

Siegel:

Risk-adjusted return is a complicated concept. The way we adjust our returns to accommodate risk is to calculate the alphas in the traditional market model, which is to say that we adjust only for the beta as measured. That probably does not do a great job with small-cap stocks because the measured betas of small-caps are too low.

An interesting paper by three of my former colleagues at Ibbotson Associates suggests a way of correcting for the understated betas of small-cap stocks. The paper, "Small Stock Betas Are Much Too Low," by Roger Ibbotson, Paul Kaplan and James Peterson, is forthcoming in the *Journal of Portfolio Management* and currently available on the World Wide Web at http:/www.ibbotson.com/ paul_beta/main.htm. The authors show that managers' alphas are lower when the beta risk of small-cap stock funds is fully accounted for. A similar adjustment may also be needed for international stock funds, which also tend to have high alphas and low betas when no adjustment is made.

A simple and useful approach to adjusting portfolio returns for total risk is proposed in "Risk-Adjusted Performance," an article written by Franco Modigliani and Leah Modigliani and published in the *Journal of Portfolio Management* (Winter 1997). Their approach is to "leverage" different portfolios by adding or subtracting cash positions (on paper) until they all have the same standard deviation. The return on these adjusted portfolios represents the risk-adjusted return on capital. We are implementing this measure for internal monitoring purposes.

For bonds, the counterpart to beta is duration and that's how we measure bond risk. We calculate a return for the bond portfolio that accounts for duration. It is conceptually an alpha. It is the extent to which you beat the index if the index has the same duration as your portfolio.

Spooner:

No, we do not adjust individual manager returns for risk. Our business, the business of investments, is to take prudent risks and to manage them at the total portfolio level. Therefore, we put considerable effort into controlling total portfolio risk through (1) diversifying our investments globally and, (2) using quantitative tools and custodian monitoring procedures to help us measure and control our total risk exposure.

Q. Are There Areas Where You Feel Your Present System Can Be Improved?

Mac Intyre:

In an ideal world, we would have a seamless data environment which would give us a "one-stop shop" for risk management so that in addition to getting a snapshot of one's holdings on a daily basis, one could generate drill-down risk reports, exception reporting, performance measurement, etc. The problem today is that each of these functions is handled, to a degree, in isolation and that creates opportunities for inconsistencies in the way we look at things. Hopefully, custodians will step up to the plate here and provide these services. The cost for plan sponsors to do this alone is prohibitive.

Siegel:

I think we would benefit in the long run from making the commitment to a portfolio holdings-based performance measurement, attribution and risk measurement system that takes a snapshot at least quarterly, and then figures out the exposures to different economic risks and enables us to do stress tests. What if interest rates went up 200 basis points and, at the same time, the Japanese stock market crashed—how much money would we lose? These things can happen; they've happened before.

It's not clear we would behave any differently if we knew the exact answer to that question. However, it's important from the plan sponsor's point of view to know what risks we are taking and how much of these risks we are taking. A "snapshot" risk measurement system could also reveal risks we don't even know we're taking. For example, risk analysis could show that we have exposure to U.S. interest rate risk in our domestic and international stock portfolios and in our bond portfolio all at the same time, in effect tripling our bet on that factor. We are in the process of evaluating the products available from various vendors and the staff commitment they require. The main issue for the Ford Foundation is not the actual cost of the product, but the time commitment to evaluate its output and put insights from using the product into practice in portfolio management.

Spooner:

We would benefit from more frequent analysis of our portfolio's specific holdings to see if our managers' investment decisions are resulting in inadvertent risk exposures. I envision a day when computer models will be readily available to perform daily VAR analysis on our total portfolio. Then perhaps we will be able to more precisely define our risk tolerance to such factors as interest rates, exchange rates, stock market volatility, etc., and take corrective action if the risks were too great.

Control and oversight of private equities and real estate are a concern. We continue to look for improved procedures to monitor the activities of our illiquid investments. Typically, the assets are not custodied with a trustee so there is a higher risk reliance on investment manager reports and analysis. For instance, while the financial statements are typically audited by a third party, the investor must rely on the investment manager to keep accounting records accurately and properly account for each investor's interests. We are continuously examining upgrades to our performance measurement and monitoring systems to incorporate new software features as they become available.

Lawson:

We're in the midst of restructuring our plan, so we've been making a great many changes. Our international exposure historically has been about 10%, but in the last two years we've gone through a complete reallocation process and have upped our international equity exposure to 25%—that's our target—and reduced our domestic equity to about 40%, so far. Our target is 35%. We're taking the fixed-income allocation up from 20% to about 30.5%. We have a global fixed-income mandate of about 13%, which is included in the 30.5% fixed-income allocation.

We don't think there are a lot of capital gains to be made in the U.S. in the near term but there's always a coupon to clip, so we use that as a safe harbor. Certainly, we have made an awful lot of money in the U.S. in the last two years and, the markets being what they are, you just have to ask yourself how long will this persist—at what point will the U.S. lose favor and see other markets outperform it?

I think any time a financial organization says we're done, it's asking for surprises. I think we always have to reinvent ourselves. We may sit and look at things and say, how could this go wrong, what could I do better? And somebody says, we're there, there's nothing else to do. About that time, something happens. Things change and you have to be willing to change with them or you accept mediocrity.

Connect yourself to THE LEADERS in:

R *eviewing standards*

I *mproving controls*

S *timulating communication*

K *nowledge & education*

MANAGEMENT

AIMA is the leading association within the global alternative investment industry.

With over 170 corporate members, its aims are to maintain high professional standards among its members, and to work with and for the end-users to ensure a full understanding and use of the management skills that have evolved within this sector.

Membership of AIMA is only achieved by recognised leaders of the industry. Therefore, you can be sure that AIMA members are among the best in the world in their area of activity.

We actively encourage communication between all areas of the industry.

Alternative Investment Management Association
The Forum for Managed Futures, Hedge Funds and Currency Management

RESOURCE GUIDE

T HE RESOURCE GUIDE IS A SERIES OF SPECIAL SECTIONS INTENDED TO ENHANCE THE EDUCATIONAL VALUE OF THIS BOOK AND EXTEND ITS USEFULNESS AS A REFERENCE TOOL AND RESOURCE.

➤ UNDERWRITER PROFILES

➤ ANNOTATED BIBLIOGRAPHY

➤ GLOSSARY

➤ APPENDIX

UNDERWRITER PROFILES

Alternative Investment Management Association (AIMA)

International House, 1 St. Katharine's Way
London, E1 9UN, England

Key Contact Information:

Florence Lombard
Executive Director   44-0171-265-3688
E-mail: florence@aima.org
Fax: 44-0171-481-8485
Internet site: http://aima.org

Year Founded: 1990

Special Areas of Expertise:

AIMA is the only true pan-European trade association promoting and lobbying on behalf of skill-based managers within the Managed Futures, Hedge Funds and Currency Management sectors.

The Association's objectives are to ensure the representation and integration of derivative and skill-based investments into mainstream fund management, and to increase investor confidence and participation in these products.

AIMA organizes educational material, sector presentations, reference publications, specified research, training events, lobbying, marketing and PR for the industry, conferences, investor forums, roundtables and institutional seminars in countries throughout Europe.

AIMA works on behalf of banks, exchanges, CTAs, CPOs, hedge fund managers, currency fund managers, brokers, prime brokers, fund managers, investors and pension funds.

Bankers Trust Company- RAROC 2020℠

130 Liberty Street, Mail Stop 2217
New York, NY 10006
Phone: 212-250-2038 • Fax: 212-250-4871

Key Contact Information:

Michelle McCarthy,
Head of Marketing and Client Service
Phone: 206-325-2020
Fax: 206-328-9055

Description of Service:

RAROC 2020℠ is an adaptation of Bankers Trust's RAROC (Risk Adjusted Return on Capital) risk measurement methodology. Institutional investors subscribe to the service to receive regular, comprehensive reporting on financial market risks across their entire portfolio. The RAROC 2020℠ service is part of Global Institutional Services at Bankers Trust, the area which provides custody and trust services for the bank's customers.

Distinguishing Features:

Instead of providing software for customers to integrate into their data systems and operate, the RAROC 2020℠ service bureau conducts the analysis for customers, receiving basic data from the custodian of the assets, and delivering the finished, highly customized risk report to the client. Customers receive state-of-the-art risk reporting without having to employ extra staff, buy software or build costly links between systems.

RAROC 2020℠ models risk at the security and portfolio level. We explicitly recognize that complex securities incorporate a variety of risks, and that these risks cut across traditional asset class boundaries. We incorporate assets with non-normally distributed returns, such as options and other complex derivatives (convertibles, mortgages, CMOs, IOs/POs, etc.), through Monte-Carlo simulation. RAROC 2020℠ draws on the correlations and volatilities of over 500 risk factors to model the portfolio holdings.

Types of Clients:

Pension plans, financial institutions, investment management firms. RAROC 2020℠ currently conducts risk reporting for more than $225 billion in assets.

Chicago Mercantile Exchange

30 S. Wacker Drive, Chicago, IL 60606
Phone: 312-930-8213 • Fax: 312-466-7466

Key Contacts:
William Kokontis, *Vice President, Marketing Programs*

Organization:
Founded in 1919, the Chicago Mercantile Exchange is the world's largest marketplace for futures and options. With its emerging markets initiative, the CME provides many new products designed to help manage risk in emerging market currencies, interest rates and equities. Some of these futures and options include the Mexican peso, Brazilian real, Mexico's IPC Stock Index, Argentine, Brazilian and Mexican Brady Bonds, the 91-day Cetes and 28-day TIIE (two Mexican interest rate products).

Product Specialties:
Currencies: Currency futures and options, in addition to those listed above, include the British pound, Deutschemark, Japanese yen, Australian and Canadian dollar and Swiss and French franc. The All-or-None feature available on all currencies allows for large orders of 100 contracts or more to be transacted at one price.

Equities: The CME offers "one-stop shopping" in the equity index futures markets, with its flagship S&P 500 contract, Mini S&P 500, NASDAQ 100, S&P MidCap 400, S&P 500/BARRA Growth Index, S&P 500/BARRA Value Index, Russell 2000® Index, Major Market Index and Nikkei 225.

Interest Rates: The CME's Eurodollar contract is the world's most actively traded futures contract. The CME also offers the one-month LIBOR, T-bill, Fed Fund, Euroyen and Euromark contracts.

GSCI Nearby Index: An index of 19 of the world's most actively traded commodities, the Goldman Sachs Commodity Index, or GSCI Nearby Index, is an alternative investment to stocks and bonds. It joins a complement of individual agricultural products, including live cattle, lean hogs, feeder cattle, pork bellies, fluid milk, butter and lumber.

Delaware Group

One Commerce Square
Philadelphia, PA 19103

Veritas House
125 Finsbury Pavement
London, England EC2A 1NQ

Key Contacts:
Barclay L. Douglas III,
Executive Vice President, Client Services
Phone: 215-255-8874 • Fax: 215-255-2954
John C.E. Campbell,
Senior Vice President, Client Services, International
Phone: 215-255-1096 • Fax: 215-255-8849

Date Founded: 1929

Organization:
Delaware Group is a full-service investment management firm that invests on behalf of institutional and mutual fund clients. Institutional investment management is the province of two units: Delaware Investment Advisers, established in 1972, which manages domestic stocks, bonds and balanced portfolios in Philadelphia, and Delaware International Advisers Ltd., formed in 1990, which manages international and global stocks, bonds and balanced portfolios in London.

Total Assets Under Management: $38.6 Billion

**Institutional Assets
Under Management:** $22.8 Billion

Distinguishing Characteristics:
• An investment style designed to produce consistent, steady returns without corresponding levels of risk or volatility over the long term.

• A team approach to portfolio management that involves more than 50 investment professionals.

• More than 230 institutional client relationships with corporate, public and Taft-Hartley plans, hospitals, endowments and foundations, among others.

• Average tenure of our client relationships is more than seven years, and almost half the relationships are more than 10 years old.

Fidelity Management Trust Company ("FMTC")

82 Devonshire Street, Boston, MA 02109

Key Contact:

Jeffrey P. Lagarce, *Sr. Vice President,*
Sales & Relationship Management   617-563-9994

Year Founded:	1982
Clients:	265
Assets Under Management:	$45.3 Billion*

*as of 6/30/97

Institutional Markets Served:

Corporate, Public, Endowment,
Foundation and Taft-Hartley

Investment Vehicles Offered:

Separately managed accounts and commingled pools

Investment Disciplines:

FMTC offers a broad array of domestic and international investment products.

Investment Approach: Throughout our product array, our common philosophy is predicated on Fidelity's 50-year commitment to fundamental bottom-up research, and the identification of investment opportunities that represent compelling values.

For all institutional capabilities, strict attention is paid to each client's investment guidelines and our investment disciplines in order to minimize style drift and meet our clients' expectations. Within their disciplines, portfolio managers are focused on consistently exceeding their benchmarks through unlimited access to Fidelity's extensive resources.

Resources: FMTC brings a depth of resources unparalleled in the investment management industry:
- more than 500 investment professionals located around the world.
- cutting-edge financial reporting, performance reporting and attribution analysis systems.
- client service professionals dedicated to meeting the needs of our institutional clients by providing value-added services.

As a privately held company, Fidelity will continue to invest in the systems, people and infrastructure necessary to stay at the forefront of the investment management business.

First Union National Bank

301 South Tryon Street, NCO362
Charlotte, NC 28288
Phone: 704-374-4621 • Fax: 704-383-6137

Key Contact Information:

Ronald Johnson,
Senior Vice President, Sales   704-374-4621

Total Assets Under Management:	$ 62.7 Billion
401(k) Assets Under Administration:	$ 11.5 Billion
Total Number of 401(k) Plans Managed:	1,302

Overview:

First Union provides Retirement and Custody Services for companies. With over $60 Billion in managed assets, we offer Administrative, Consultative, Communication/Education and Investment Management services for your Plan.

Holl International LLC

433 California Street, Suite 600
San Francisco, CA 94104

Key Contacts:

Steven G. Rubenstein,
Arrow Partners - Marketing   212-233-0411

Eric J. Fry, *President and
Chief Investment Officer*   415-986-6260

P. Edward Holl, *Chairman
and Senior Portfolio Manager*   415-391-3332

Year Founded: 1992

Total Assets Under Management: $100 Million

Profile: Holl International is a privately owned, independent investment advisory firm which manages money for institutional and individual investors. Its principals are highly qualified professionals with extensive backgrounds in investment research and international portfolio management.

Holl focuses on countries, sectors and companies not commonly found through other core international managers, making it a perfect complement to your money manager line up.

Objective: Holl provides investors with a concentrated, value-driven, non-correlated international equity portfolio that achieves performance superior to major international equity indices. We identify emerging economic trends that indicate a market's potential for excess performance. Within markets we identify significant undervalued securities. We capitalize on the most attractive and rare international equity opportunities through rigorous and disciplined research.

Philosophy: Compelling opportunities emerge when favorable macro-trends converge upon discounted equity market valuations.

Process: Our "top-down" investment approach identifies international markets or sectors poised for superior performance. Initial analysis focuses upon regional economic development and the capital flows which influence economies and markets. We then analyze the prevailing monetary and liquidity conditions relative to market valuations and price trends. Finally, we conduct security-level research to select the most compelling beneficiary of anticipated trends. Our network of foreign contacts provides critical local insights and conducts behind-the-scenes due diligence when required. The decision to buy (or sell) results from an inner-portfolio "competition for capital." Capital is allocated and withdrawn according to each security's evolving risk/return profile.

Independence Investment Associates, Inc. and Subsidiary

53 State Street, Boston, MA 02109

Key Contacts:

Derek Hepworth, C.F.A.,
Senior Vice President
Phone: 617-228-8760 • Fax: 617-228-8819

Year Founded: 1982

Type of Organization:
Independent Investment Counselor
Registered Investment Advisor

Assets Under Management: $26.8 Billion
as of 6/30/97

Introduction:
Independence Investment Associates, Inc. offers domestic and international equity and domestic fixed-income management services in the institutional marketplace. As an active quantitative manager, Independence employs innovative investment technology and focused fundamental research to identify opportunities arising from mispricing of individual securities to deliver maximum investment performance within client-specified risk parameters.

Philosophy:
Across disciplines, we seek to identify securities which have the best combination of cheapness and improving fundamentals.

Decision-Making Process:
Using fundamental estimates from our research group to drive our Multifactor Valuation Model, we generate a daily ranking of all securities in our universe. Portfolios are constructed from our ranked list of securities and optimized to a client-specified benchmark. Portfolio strategy is geared toward maximizing expected return while maintaining market-like risk and low volatility.

Investment Strategies:
U.S. Equities:
Core, Growth, Value, Medium-Cap, Market Neutral, Amplified Alpha, and REITs.

Fixed-Income:
Core, Custom Benchmark, Synthetic GIC

International Equities:
EAFE, Global, Emerging Markets

Instinet Corporation
875 Third Ave., New York, NY 10022

Key Contact:
Scott Florio, *Sales Manager*   800-874-0039

Year Founded: 1969

The Company:
Instinet Corporation, a subsidiary of Reuters Holdings PLC, and its broker-dealer affiliates, provide agency brokerage services in global equities to securities industry professionals in over 30 countries, delivered primarily through sophisticated computer technology. Instinet provides its equity transaction and research services to a global base of institutional fund managers and plan sponsors, other brokers, dealers and exchange specialists. Instinet was acquired by Reuters in 1987, and now has offices in eight key financial centers worldwide.

Instinet, collectively with its affiliates, is a member of the National Association of Securities Dealers; all U.S. regional exchanges; the American Stock Exchange; the Toronto, London, Paris, Zurich, Hong Kong, Frankfurt, and Stockholm Exchanges; the Chicago Board Options Exchange; and the European Options Exchange (Amsterdam); and is a registered Broker/Dealer in Tokyo.

As an agency broker, Instinet remains neutral in its transactions, neither buying nor selling securities for its own account. Its only business is providing brokerage services for the benefit of its customers through its innovative application of computer and communications technology. For Instinet's customers, the primary benefit of using Instinet as their broker is the ability to reduce trading, or transaction costs, and, in doing so, improve investment performance.

Services Offered:
Trading:
• Equity Trading
• List Trading
• Crossing Services

Research:
• Research and Analytics
• Soft Commissions
• Transactions Analysis

John Hancock Funds
A Global Investment Management Firm
101 Huntington Avenue, Boston, MA 02199
Phone: 800-755-4371 • Fax: 617-375-4710

Key Contact:
James V. Bowhers,
Executive Vice President   617-375-4880

Year Founded: 1968

Total Assets Under Management: $27 Billion*
**as of 6/30/97*

Organization:
John Hancock Funds is a subsidiary of John Hancock Financial Services, one of the nation's leading financial services providers. With over $110 billion in assets under management, John Hancock has been providing financial security for customers since 1862. In today's complex financial environment, John Hancock is able to demonstrate exceptional financial strength to customers who expect the highest possible financial security and integrity. With more than $51 billion in institutional assets under management, John Hancock has been a leader in the institutional marketplace for over 50 years.

John Hancock Funds' Institutional Investments & Services group offers a full range of investment management and client services for institutional investors, including institutional mutual funds, commingled pools and separate account management.

Investment Approach:
The same investment management philosophy upon which our organization was founded is still firmly in place today. Our investment strategies all share this common philosophy:
• Total Team Approach to Portfolio Management and Research
• Disciplined Investment Process
• Focused Fundamental Research

We have broad expertise covering fixed-income and equity markets both domestically and abroad.

Active Equity Management:	*Active Fixed-Income Management:*
Global and Domestic	Small, Mid & Large-Cap
Enhanced Core	Value
High-Yield	Growth
	International

MetLife

One Madison Avenue, New York, NY 10010

Key Contact:
Eugene Marks, Jr.,
Vice President-Institutional Sales   212-578-0300

Year Founded: 1868
mutual insurance company since 1915

**Total Assets
Under Management:** $300 Billion*

**Total Tax-Exempt Assets
Under Management:** $90.8 Billion*
* as of 12/31/96

Overview: MetLife offers a wide variety of guaranteed products and commingled and separately managed fixed-income, equity, real estate and global accounts available through group annuity contracts. MetLife's thousands of institutional clients include ERISA, non-ERISA, public, Taft-Hartley, for-profit and not-for-profit entities. Drawing from a wide variety of financial strategies, our professionals provide fully integrated investment and service solutions for clients.

Wholly Owned Investment Management Subsidiaries: State Street Research & Management Company actively manages domestic equity and fixed-income and global and international fixed-income accounts. GFM International Investors Limited specializes in core international equity management. SSR Realty Advisors offers select real estate investment strategies for apartment, retail, office and industrial properties through separate accounts, private REITs and advisory programs including co-investments. MetLife's Investment Departments provide passive equity management, money market and short-term index guaranteed funds. MetLife also provides guaranteed contracts, including guarantees linked to various fixed-income indices.

Investment Alliance: MetLife offers a publicly traded real estate investment capability through a strategic alliance with EII Realty Securities, Inc.

Separate Account Annuities: MetLife is widely recognized as a market leader in the design and implementation of innovative annuity solutions for large pension plans. The Met Managed Annuity provides MetLife's guarantees for participant benefits, quality investment management and the protection of a segregated separate account.

Morgan Grenfell Asset Management Ltd.

885 Third Avenue, New York, NY 10022

Key Contacts:
Christopher Thorsheim, *SVP*   212-230-2607
Fred Devlin, *EVP*   212-230-2643
Martin Hall, *EVP*   215-418-3068

Year founded: 1838 (U.S. presence since 1977)

Assets Under Management:
as of 6/30/97

Worldwide Clients: 2,680   Assets: $141 Billion
North American Clients: 248   Assets: $25 Billion

Investment Offices: New York, Philadelphia, London, Frankfurt, Tokyo, Singapore and Hong Kong.

Overview: Morgan Grenfell is comprised of four investment teams: U.S. Fixed-Income, Global Fixed-Income, U.S. Small-Cap Equity and International Equity. In many instances client mandates allow for the utilization of more than one of these teams' investment expertise.

The U.S. Fixed-Income team manages core taxable and tax-exempt municipal bond accounts. Morgan Grenfell uses a bottom-up approach emphasizing fundamental credit research to identify the most attractive, high-quality issues in the U.S. bond market.

The Global Fixed-Income team manages global, non-U.S. and emerging debt portfolios. Our core global process identifies relative value between countries and currencies with an emphasis on sovereign debt instruments. *The Emerging Markets Debt* team's process focuses on both country and issue selection.

The U.S. Small-Cap Equity team manages small and micro-cap portfolios. The process is bottom-up and growth-oriented. Our stock research is conducted by portfolio managers who specialize in particular sectors of the market. Company visits are the most important source of information in the investment process.

The International Equity team offers core regional, small-cap and emerging markets capabilities to institutional clients. In-house company research derived through company visits dominates the investment process with less reliance on top-down regional decisions. Superior stock selection is a priority and will lead to more consistent performance.

Rogers, Casey & Associates, Inc.

One Parklands Drive, Darien, CT 06820
Phone: 203-656-5900 • Fax: 203-656-2233

1995 University Avenue, Berkeley, CA 94707
Phone: 510-704-5060 • Fax: 510-548-1965

Key Contacts:
William W. Kelly, *Managing Director*   203-656-5983
Lisa B. Stanton, *Managing Director*   510-704-5061

Year Founded: 1976; wholly owned
subsidiary of BARRA, Inc.

Business Mission:
Rogers, Casey & Associates, Inc. offers products and services designed for the investment programs of institutional investors.

The firm combines BARRA's advanced technology with professional relationship management to deliver investment tools, consulting and special assets advisory (multiple-manager programs).

Clients:
RogersCasey services 150 institutional investor clients—corporate and public funds, endowments, foundations, hospitals, law firms, insurance companies and unions—with over $500 billion in assets.

Services:
RogersCasey Sponsor Services provides investment tools and professional services to assist investors with the following issues:
• Asset Allocation
• Investment Structure Design
• Manager/Vendor Selection
• Performance Measurement
• Plan-Wide Risk Assessment

RogersCasey Asset Services manages multiple-manager investment programs such as separate-account mandates across all asset classes and commingled vehicles, including emerging markets and market neutral strategies.

Index to Underwriters

ANNOTATED BIBLIOGRAPHY

RECOMMENDATIONS FROM THE AUTHORS AND INVESTORS PRESS

BOOKS

Global Investment Risk Management: Managing Against Currency, Interest Rate, Equity and Commodity Risk, by Ezra Zask (Burr Ridge, IL: Irwin Professional Publishing, 1997). A guide to understanding and managing global investment risk. Topics include emerging market investments, derivative risk management and currency as an asset class.

The following five books, published in 1996, are available from the Association for Investment Management and Research (AIMR), Charlottesville, VA. Call (800) 789-AIMR.

Global Equity Investing discusses the opportunities and challenges faced by portfolio managers investing in developing countries and explores equity strategies "with a global or distinctly regional flavor."

Global Portfolio Management identifies the fundamental components of global portfolio management, focusing on investment policy and expectations, asset allocation and implementation, and performance measurement.

Investing Worldwide VI examines the widening spectrum of risks incurred through global investment and examines strategies for identifying, quantifying and managing these risks.

Investing Worldwide VII: Focus on Emerging Markets discusses techniques for conducting research and managing risk in emerging market securities and also presents strategies for managing portfolios composed of emerging market equity and fixed-income securities.

Currency Management: Concepts and Practices is a tutorial focusing on the fundamental concepts and mathematics of exchange rates and currency management. This book shows readers how currency management can be used to reduce risk and enhance returns.

ARTICLES AND PERIODICALS

Note: The following *Global Investor* and *Euromoney* articles can be accessed on the Internet at: www.euromoney.com.

➤ *Currency Hedging and Derivatives*
"The Case for Currency Overlay," by Simon Brady, *Global Investor,* February 1996, Cover Story. According to the author, currency should be treated as a separate asset class. This article explains how to manage currency as an overlay and discusses the strengths and weaknesses of two commonly used currency risk management strategies—dynamic hedging and active currency management.

"Cautious Investors Seek Safety," by Mariana Crespo, *Euromoney*, June 1996, pp. 222-224. Many corporations investing in developing countries are using derivatives as a means of risk management. Commonly used products include Brady bond options, structured notes, and cross-currency interest rate swaps, which can be used to lower borrowing costs in these markets.

"Investment Policy Implications of Currency Hedging," by Kenneth J. Winston and Jeffrey V. Bailey, *The Journal of Portfolio Management*, Summer 1996, pp. 50-57. Presents an alternative approach to hedging the currency exposure of a fund's allocation to international stocks. The authors find that increasing a fund's allocation to domestic assets and decreasing its allocation to unhedged international stocks can achieve comparable risk reduction effects to those of hedging, while eliminating the financial and administrative expenses of a currency hedging program.

➤ *Country Risk Measures*

Note: Campbell Harvey, co-author of the articles below, has published his study of "Country Risk Analysis" on the Internet at: www.duke.edu/~charvey/Country_risk/couindex.htm.

"Expected Returns and Volatility in 135 Countries," by Claude B. Erb, Campbell R. Harvey and Tadas E. Viskanta, *The Journal of Portfolio Management*, Spring 1996, pp. 46-59. Using credit risk "as a single explanatory variable," the authors calculate the expected returns and volatilities in 135 different markets. Given each country's predicted country risk premium and volatility, the authors calculate the number of years it would take an investor to double his initial investment in each country with 90% probability.

"The Influence of Political, Economic, and Financial Risk on Expected Fixed-Income Returns," by Claude B. Erb, Campbell R. Harvey and Tadas E. Viskanta, *Journal of Fixed Income*, June 1996, pp. 7-30. Fixed-income investment strategies based on publicly available measures of political, financial and economic risk can produce positive, risk-adjusted returns. In addition, the authors find a substantial correlation between country risk measures and international bond measures, such as real yields.

"Political Risk, Economic Risk, and Financial Risk," by Claude B. Erb, Campbell R. Harvey and Tadas E. Viskanta, *Financial Analysts Journal*, November/December 1996. Political, economic and financial measures of country risk provide valuable financial insight and are significantly correlated with equity valuation measures, such as price-to-book ratios. The authors postulate that this correlation is an important factor in explaining why value-oriented strategies generate high average returns.

➤ *Global Investment Strategies*

"Explaining Premiums and Discounts on Closed-End Equity Country Funds," by Bala Arshanapalli, Jongmo Jay Choi, E. Tyler Clagget, Jr., John Doukas and Insup Lee, *Journal of Applied Corporate Finance*, Fall 1996, pp. 109-117. Explains why the prices of closed-end equity country funds (or ECFs) are highly volatile, often trading higher or lower than the underlying net asset values. The authors also evaluate the efficiency of ECFs as vehicles for international diversification.

"A Global Stock and Bond Model," by Lucie Chaumeton, Gregory Connor, and Ross Curds, *Financial Analysts Journal*, November/December 1996. Provides a model of global stock and bond returns that can be used to integrate global asset selection and asset allocation decisions. This model has six factors: "shift and twist factors for bonds; market, size, value, and duration factors for stocks."

"A Practical Approach to Calculating Costs of Equity for Investments in Emerging Markets," by Stephen Godfrey and Ramon Espinosa, *Journal of Applied Corporate Finance*, Fall 1996, pp. 80-89. When calculating the net present value of prospective investments, projected cash flows are discounted at a risk-adjusted rate. It can be extremely difficult, however, to determine the appropriate discount rate for emerging market investments because of the wide variety of risks, such as political risk and currency exposure. This paper proposes a viable framework for determining the proper discount rate.

"Should Japan Be Underweighted in a Non-U.S. Equity Benchmark?" by Ernest M. Ankrim and Grant W. Gardner, *Journal of Portfolio Management*, Winter 1996, pp. 9-17. The authors explore possible justifications for a non-U.S. equity benchmark that underweights Japan and explain how even a small underweighting can result in significant under-performance of a standard, fully weighted non-U.S. equity benchmark.

➤ Risk Management Strategies

"Evaluation of Value-at-Risk Models Using Historical Data," by Darryll Hendricks, *Economic Policy Review*, April 1996, pp. 39-69. This article studies the performance of 12 value-at-risk models on 1,000 randomly chosen foreign exchange portfolios. Evaluating model performance on nine specific criteria, the author finds that, overall, the approaches generate risk estimates of similar average size.

"Foreign Exchange Markets: Structures and Systemic Risks," by Laura E. Kodres, *Finance & Development*, December 1996. Failure to execute a single foreign exchange settlement can disrupt global financial markets. This article proposes various mechanisms to manage the systemic risks posed by cross-border settlements. Access via: www.worldbank.org/fandd/english/1296/dec96.htm.

"Global Financial Markets: Moving Up the Learning Curve," by the International Monetary Fund Research Department Staff, *Finance & Development*, December 1996. Costly global market crises have caused international financial market participants to learn from past mistakes and find new ways to better manage the private and systemic risks in those markets. Access via the Internet at: www.worldbank.org/fandd/english/1296/dec96.htm.

"Managing Market Exposure," by Robert B. Litterman and Kurt D. Winkelman, *Journal of Portfolio Management*, Summer 1996, pp. 32-48. Risk management has become much more complex in recent years due to the increased prevalence of foreign securities and derivatives. The authors explain how a new risk management technique called "market exposure" can help portfolio managers predict how their portfolios will perform in market rallies.

"Managing the Risk of Your Global Bond Portfolio," by Kieran Higgins, *Global Investor,* April 1996, Cover Story. Traditional risk measurement techniques may be inadequate for managing global bond portfolios, as they behave very differently from those of domestic bonds. This article discusses the challenges of quantifying and controlling the market risk of a global bond portfolio relative to a benchmark.

➤ *Global Custody*

Global Custodian, published quarterly by Asset International in Greenwich, CT, offers custody and agent bank surveys, as well as coverage of important custodial issues, such as clearance and settlement of emerging market transactions. Call (203) 629-5014.

"Is Small Beautiful?" by Tim Hyam, *Global Investor,* May 1996, Cover Story. Do small custodians provide a higher level of customer service and specialization than their larger counterparts? This article presents *Global Investor's* "Global Custody Survey 1996," and discusses the survey's methodology and results. Note: Look for *Global Investor's* May 1997 issue for results of its 1997 survey.

"USA: Going Native," by Stephen Davis, *Institutional Investor,* January 30, 1997, p. 141. Discusses the recent trend in which global custodians hire local, unaffiliated subcustodians in emerging market nations. Includes a ranking of global custodians based on total global custody assets.

WEB SITES

Campbell R. Harvey: Country Risk Analysis, (www.duke.edu/~charvey/Country_risk/couindex.htm). Duke University Professor Campbell Harvey's extensive study of political, financial and economic risk, and the behavior of emerging market returns.

Euromoney World Link, (www.euromoney.com). Access to current and archived issues of *Euromoney* Publications, PLC, including complete coverage of *Euromoney* and *World Link* and selected issues of *Global Investor.*

Ibbotson's Library, (www.ibbotson.com/research.htm). Contains insightful investment research provided by Ibbotson Associates. Below are two interesting articles that can be found at this site:

"The $40 Trillion Market: Global Stock and Bond Capitalizations and Returns," by Laurence B. Siegel. Presents the market capitalization and historical returns of publicly traded stocks and bonds in a broad sample of developed and emerging national markets. The author discusses the implications of his findings, as they relate to the expected future returns on stocks and bonds and the effectiveness of international diversification as a means of reducing investment correlation.

"Stocks, Brady Bonds, and Currencies: Investment Opportunities in Latin America," by Paul D. Kaplan. Opportunities for foreign investment in Latin American capital markets have greatly increased in recent years, due in part to the creation of Brady bonds and related derivative contracts. In an attempt to quantify these investment opportunities, this article provides data on Latin American equity indices, Brady bonds and currencies.

Morgan Stanley Capital International, (www.ms.com/mscidata/index.html). Offers daily reports on selected MSCI indices, including the EAFE index. Morgan Stanley is making this site available to the public on a trial basis through December 31, 1997.

The Risk Standards Working Group, (www.cmra.com). Led by Tanya Styblo Beder and Maarten Nederlof of Capital Market Risk Advisors, Inc., with representation from leading plan sponsors. The group created seminal "Risk Standards for Institutional Investment Managers and Institutional Investors" to help the investment industry understand, measure, monitor and control risk. (See Appendix.)

The World Bank Group, (www.worldbank.org). Features worthwhile, rigorously researched articles that are highly regarded by leading emerging markets money managers. Includes in-depth country and region reports, as well as full online publication of *Finance and Development*.

SUGGESTIONS FROM THE UNDERWRITERS

Bankers Trust Company/RAROC 2020^{SM} suggests the following articles:

"Value at Risk in an Investment Management Business: Enhancing the Control Framework," by Michelle McCarthy, *Bank Accounting & Finance*, Vol. 10, No. 4, Summer 1997, p. 17. Explains how investment firm managers can use value-at-risk measures to supervise risk-taking and compares them to existing tools.

"Topics in Corporate Risk Management: An End-User's Perspective," by David Shimko, a series of 24 monthly articles originally published in *Risk Magazine* between 1995 and 1997. Includes features on how investors and corporations can use value-at-risk measures to better manage their financial risks.

Contact Margaret Rawson at 212-250-9321.

Fidelity recommends:

"The Outlook for Active International Equity Management," presented at the Institute for International Research conference, New York City, October, 1989. Contact Edward E. Madden, Vice Chairman at 617-563-6144.

Holl International suggests the following resources. For more information, contact Steven Rubenstein at 212-233-0411.

International Investing with ADRs —Your Passport to Profits Worldwide, by Eric J. Fry, Chief Investment Officer, 1994. The first comprehensive guide to investing internationally with American Depository Receipts.

"Bargains at a Discount," *Grant's Asia Observer*, June 23, 1997.

"Passage to India," *Grant's Interest Rate Observer*, April 11, 1997.

"Pro Euro-Value," *Grant's Interest Rate Observer*, October 25, 1996.

"The World is Your Oyster," *Business Week*, December 30, 1996-January 6, 1997.

"Yield is No Object," *Grant's Asia Observer*, November 25, 1996.

Independence Investment Associates, Inc. recommends three articles published by David A. Umstead and a fourth published by Umstead and his colleagues:

"The Portfolio Management Process," published in **Initiating and Managing a Global Investment Program** (Charlottesville, VA: AIMR, 1991). A description of the key ingredients to successful global investing, covering benchmarks, philosophy, country selection, stock selection and currency hedging.

"Selecting a Benchmark for International Investments," *Financial Analysts Journal,* March/April 1990. A brief discussion of the unique difficulties in selecting an international equity benchmark with simple, common sense solutions.

"International Equity Style Management," published in **Equity Style Management** (Burr Ridge, IL: Irwin Professional Publishing, 1995). A focus on Independence International Associates' style indices and the method used to construct the indices and performance data for the Europe-Pacific region. The data shows a pronounced tendency for the cheap half of most markets to outperform the expensive half. Umstead demonstrates the importance of country diversification and presents a useful study of the interaction between rebalancing interval, transaction costs and performance.

"Style Indexes: Powerful Tools for Building Global Stock-Selection Models," published in **Quantitative Investing for the Global Markets: Strategies, Tactics, and Advanced Analytical Techniques** (Chicago, IL: Glenlake Publishing Co. and Fitzroy Dearborn Publishers, 1997). Umstead collaborates with Independence colleagues Michael McElroy, David Shea and Dennis Fogarty to test a variety of stock selection models. Each of the models are used to create a set of style indexes and compare and contrast performance.

MetLife recommends the following two internally produced articles. Fax requests to Mark Foley at 212-578-5730.

"Asset Allocation Decisions & Annuity Purchases," discusses the effects of various investment strategies on reaching or maintaining full funding, and explores different approaches for plan sponsors to achieve their goals.

"Why Liabilities Matter" highlights several often overlooked aspects of pension plan management that can have a critical impact on a plan's operations. A real life case study illustrates the importance of ongoing liability management.

RogersCasey suggests the following two reports. Contact Karen Dehmel at 203-656-5947.

"Plan-Wide Risk Analysis: Methodology and Case Studies," by Ronald Kahn, Chris J. Cesare and Drew W. Demakis. Describes the methodology for aggregating risks across BARRA's single country bond and stock models to arrive at measures of total plan risk and active plan risk, including volatilites and value-at-risk (VAR). Illustrates applications of plan-wide risk analysis, such as manager structure design, guideline development, portfolio rebalancing and trade-offs through a series of case studies.

"Non-U.S. Bonds: An Opportunistic Versus Dedicated Approach," by Drew W. Demakis and Robert E. Capaldi, *Journal of Pension Plan Investing*, Fall 1996. Examines in detail the empirical evidence of the incremental contribution of non-dollar bonds to institutional portfolios and discusses implementation issues regarding the allocation to non-U.S. bonds. The authors find that the inclusion of non-U.S. bonds as a separate asset class contributes very little to the overall risk and return of the portfolio, and suggest that they be viewed as another sector within the fixed-income markets.

GLOSSARY

Active Management: A broad class of management in which the manager's portfolio decisions are based on valuation and judgment, rather than on replicating a benchmark.

Alpha: The risk-adjusted excess return (positive or negative) of an asset relative to its benchmark. For a detailed, technical explanation of alpha, see William F. Sharpe, Gordon J. Alexander and Jeffrey V. Bailey, **Investments**, 5th Edition (Englewood Cliffs, NJ: Prentice Hall, 1995).

Asset Allocation: The process of determining the optimum asset mix for a portfolio; universally considered the determining factor in long-term portfolio performance.

Basis Point: One hundredth of one percent, a convenient measure of securities price or yield. The difference in yield between an 8.25% bond and a 8.50% bond is 25 basis points.

Benchmark: A performance standard used as a basis for comparison. The performance of a fund manager is often compared to a predetermined benchmark that reflects the manager's trading style. In some cases, a standard index, such as the S&P 500 may be used; in other cases, the benchmark may be a custom-made combination of indices.

Beta: A coefficient that measures a stock's volatility relative to the stock market as a whole. The S&P 500 Index has a beta of 1; a stock with a higher beta is more volatile than the market and one with a lower beta is less volatile than the market.

Book Value: A measure of a security's value upon liquidation. Book value can differ greatly from market value, which indicates a security's current market price at the time of measurement.

Closed-End Mutual Fund: A publicly traded mutual fund that sells a fixed number of shares on stock exchanges or over-the-counter. In contrast to open-end mutual funds, closed-end funds do not continuously issue and redeem their shares. Typically, the funds are specialized in terms of asset types and/or objectives. For example, the Korea Fund, listed on the New York Stock Exchange, concentrates on Korean equities.

Compliance Risk: The possibility that existing procedures do not adequately ensure that the plan and its managers adhere to the regulations and requirements of governmental and regulatory bodies and industry standards of practice or that the recordkeeping of compliance documentation is not sufficient to show that the plan and its managers have been in compliance.

Contrarian View: A view that is opposite to that of most investors. For example, a contrarian investor may purchase out-of-favor asset classes or securities, such as stocks with low price/earnings ratios.

Corporate (Financial) Risk: The potential that events and/or decisions at the plan will have an adverse impact on the financial statements of the corporation, e.g., the ability to maintain adequate funding for the plan.

Correlation: The relationship between the returns of one asset class or investment and those of another. Common stocks and venture capital, for example, both represent corporate equity and correlate more closely than do common stocks and Treasury bills. One objective of asset diversification is to reduce correlation, so that when the value of one asset is declining, the value of the other is rising. A statistical measure of this relationship is called the "correlation coefficient".

Counterparty Risk: The risk that the other party in a transaction will default, thereby failing to complete the agreement. In an options agreement, for example, it is the risk to the option buyer that the option seller will fail to execute the transaction (i.e., buy or sell the underlying security as agreed) in the event the option is exercised.

Coverage Ratios: Ratios used to test the adequacy of a corporation's profits for meeting debt and lease obligations. Coverage ratios measure a company's margin of safety. Examples include the interest coverage ratio and the fixed charge coverage ratio.

Currency Risk: The underlying investment risk in securities of, or investments in, a foreign country denominated in the local currency. Foreign exchange fluctuations make the currency's value volatile, thus affecting the value of the security (its net gain or loss). Currency risk must be factored into the total return calculation of an international investment. Many investors hedge currency risk through currency futures or options.

Custodian: A financial institution that handles numerous custodial, clearance and related administrative functions on behalf of its clients. The custody process involves: safekeeping responsibility (ensuring good title to the securities), security transfer and clearance for transactions and settlement, accounting for all transactions, collection of dividends and interest, and possible reinvestment of these proceeds.

Derivatives: Tradable instruments based on an underlying security or commodity. Options and futures, for example, are based on stocks, bonds, currencies and indices and are not the responsibility of the issuer. Other derivatives, such as mortgage-backed securities and CMOs (collateralized mortgage obligations), are the issuers' responsibility.

Dividend Discount Model: A mathematical model used to determine a stock's value (the price it "should" be selling at). The model is calculated from the discounted value of the stock's projected future dividend payments.

Duration: Generally, a measure of the sensitivity of an instrument or portfolio to the movement of interest rates. Originally, it was applied only to fixed-income instruments as a means of characterizing the impact of interest rate changes on bond price movements; today, it is used for equities, real estate and other asset classes, as well. Technically, duration is the midpoint of the present value of all income generated by a security held to maturity (assuming all cash flows are reinvested): it is the number of years required to receive the present value of future payments, both interest and principal, from a security or investment. Duration changes as a result of changing interest rates, and also as a security or investment approaches maturity.

EAFE Index (Europe and Australasia, Far East Equity Index): An international stock index calculated by the Morgan Stanley Capital International group. The EAFE index is often used as a benchmark for global stock portfolios.

Equity Index Options: Options on stock indexes. Equity index options allow traders to speculate on particular market segments without having to buy all the stocks represented in the index.

Fiduciary Risk: The potential exposure of the plan fiduciaries to legal and regulatory actions precipitated by a breakdown in controls, or the failure to execute due diligence on behalf of the plans.

Futures Contract: A binding agreement between two parties to deliver or accept delivery of a specified commodity or financial instrument at a preset price and future date. These agreements are standardized with respect to the type and amount of the asset, as well as to the times and places of delivery. Traders buy and sell futures in order to manage their risk or to make a profit.

Growth Manager: A portfolio manager who buys the stocks of corporations which have shown rapid earnings increases in recent years, and which are expected to continue to have high growth in profits. Growth stocks usually outperform slower growing stocks, but they are riskier because they have a higher price/earnings ratio and make little or no dividend payments to shareholders. The objective of a growth strategy is to provide long-term capital appreciation.

Hedging: A trading strategy which involves taking an offsetting position to reduce risk or limit loss. For example, a hedger might take one of the following positions: buy (own) an asset and sell the corresponding futures contracts or sell (owe) a physical commodity and buy an equal number of the corresponding futures contracts. Global portfolio managers often hedge currency risk by selling futures contracts of the same underlying currency.

Information Ratio: The ratio of active return to active risk annualized. The information ratio can be used as an indicator of a manager's opportunity to add value. Theoretically, the most skillful managers will have the highest information ratios.

Leverage: An investment strategy that allows an investor to control a large amount of assets with a minimal investment. In some cases, an investor may use borrowed funds to acquire assets. In other cases, leverage can be achieved through the purchase of options and futures contracts, which give the investor control of the underlying assets. Leverage is a double-edged sword: it can increase profits or it can exaggerate losses.

Liquidity Risk: The possible failure to maintain sufficient funds (cash and marketable securities) to meet short-term obligations. Also, market liquidity risk is the difficulty in liquidating certain investments due to the lack of active markets in these securities.

Index: A statistical measure of the value of a group of securities selected to represent a market or market segment. Common examples include the Dow Jones Industrial Average, a price-weighted average of 30 blue-chip stocks, and Standard & Poor's 500 Index, a market value-weighted index of 500 stocks.

Macroeconomic Conditions: Aggregate economic factors affecting the economy as a whole, such as price levels, inflation and unemployment.

Managed Futures: Investment vehicles managed by professional investment managers who participate in global futures market trading. The levels of diversification can range from specialized market sector concentrations to completely diversified portfolios.

Mark to Market: The market value of an instrument or portfolio at a given point in time. Typically, this term is used to describe a valuation at a time other than the time of purchase or sale. Because this is not necessarily a transaction price, it is not necessarily representative of the value upon liquidation, which might suffer from market impact and other transaction costs.

Market Risk: The possibility of loss due to large movements in market prices (e.g., due to changes in interest rates, foreign exchange rates, volatility, correlations between markets, capital flows).

Modeling Risk: The potential for loss due to actions taken or to policies implemented based on views of the world, in general, and the investment community, in particular, that are derived from improper models. These views are derived from representation(s) of reality that do not capture all significantly relevant information or are inappropriately applied throughout the investment program.

Modern Portfolio Theory: A theoretical approach to quantifying risk and return in a portfolio of stocks. It emphasizes the portfolio rather than individual securities and, in particular, how securities perform (or affect risk) in relation to each other. Developed in 1959 by Harry Markowitz, MPT is the foundation for present-day principles of investment diversification.

Normal Distribution: A probability distribution used for statistical analysis. Shown graphically, a normal distribution appears as a symmetrical, bell-shaped curve with a single peak (the mean or average) at the center of the distribution. Using a normal distribution, statisticians can make certain assumptions about the predicted range of values based on a sample's standard deviation.

Operational Risk: The potential for discontinuity due to the possibility of a breakdown in operational procedures particularly as they relate to a process breakdown. This is distinct from the design, implementation and maintenance of computerized information systems, e.g., errors resulting from a lack of reviewer functions to catch errors, from incorrect data and/or lack of adequate staffing/backup.

Optimization Process: A mathematical technique used to create "optimal" mixes of asset classes. Generally, an optimal asset mix is one that produces the maximum expected return at a given level of risk or a minimum level of risk at a given level of return.

Option: A contract between two parties which grants the bearer the right, without obligation, to buy or sell a specified asset at a fixed price (called the "strike price") until a preset date. In return for the option, the option buyer must pay the option seller a premium. There are two basic kinds of options: "calls" and "puts". A call is the right to buy the underlying asset at the option's strike price. A put is the right to sell the underlying asset at the option's strike price. Call option holders hope that the market price of the underlying asset will increase above the option's strike price, while put option holders hope that the price will decrease below the option's strike price.

Overlay Program: Adding a portfolio of derivatives, typically futures or forward contracts, to an existing portfolio. Because these derivative instruments require little or no initial capital outlay, they can be "overlaid" on top of an existing portfolio without disrupting capital allocation. Currency overlays are often used to add currency exposure to a portfolio or to hedge a portfolio's currency risk.

Passive Management: A broad class of management, utilizing such vehicles as index funds and dedicated portfolios. Once the portfolio is structured, there is theoretically no subsequent management, other than rebalancing. A less expensive investment approach, adopted in cases when it's doubtful that active management can add value or unnecessary for it to do so.

Performance Attribution: Analysis of the factors affecting a money manager's performance. Performance attribution analysis seeks to identify the major sources of value-added, and to determine whether market timing, short-term factor timing and security selection were statistically significant.

Plain Vanilla Instrument: The most common form of interest rate swap. In such a swap, one party agrees to pay a fixed rate of interest, while the other pays according to a floating rate, such as LIBOR. Payments are based on an agreed-upon principal amount (called the "notational principal amount"); however, only interest payments are exchanged in the transaction. Interest rate swaps can be used to synthetically alter the duration of an asset or liability.

Quantitative Approach: A type of securities analysis that examines a corporation's financial data, including its assets, liabilities, sales patterns and profitability. Quantitative analysts often use computer programs to analyze large amounts of data to predict a security's future price movements.

Rebalancing: The process of adjusting a portfolio's holdings (or factor exposure) to equal a desired exposure. For example: if a portfolio has a target investment allocation of 50% equities and 50% cash but, due to market movements, has a current allocation of 55% equities and 45% cash, rebalancing would move 5% of the portfolio from equities to cash so that the actual portfolio holdings equal the target investment allocation.

Resistance Point: Price level at which selling tends to take place, according to technical analysis of a security's price history.

Risk Relative to Benchmark: The potential for losses due to unintended bets or a break-down in due diligence: the impact of investment initiatives that were not fully understood at the outset and had the potential of unintended consequences or the monetary impact (to the portfolio and the fund) of managers who violate guidelines, engage in unauthorized transactions, develop excessive concentrations (high tracking error), fraud, etc.

Risk Tolerance: The amount of risk or variability an investor is willing to accept in exchange for additional reward in the form of a higher expected return. Investors who demand a higher reward in exchange for an increase in risk have a lower risk tolerance than those who demand a lower reward.

Securities Lending: A transaction in which brokers (including banks and custodians with broker status) lend securities from their inventory to a customer making a short sale for delivery to the buying customer's broker. The borrowing broker deposits with the lending broker a cash amount equal to the market value of the securities as collateral. Securities lending is analogous to a bank making its loans with customer deposits and is a lucrative and important business activity for financial institutions. Customers whose securities are lent (large pension funds, for example) often share the income generated from such transactions, thereby offsetting investment management and custodial costs. The SEC requires that brokers obtain permission from their customers to have their securities used in loan transactions; this is requested in the standard agreement customers sign when they open general accounts.

Sharpe Ratio: A statistical measure used to determine a portfolio's reward relative to its total variability. Developed by Nobel Laureate William Sharpe, the Sharpe ratio is calculated using standard deviation and "excess return", a measure of a portfolio's return in comparison to that of a risk-free investment. The Sharpe Ratio represents a portfolio's excess return per unit of risk. The higher the ratio, the better the portfolio's risk-adjusted performance.

Short Selling: Selling an asset which one does not own. For example, a trader may sell the long bond if he believes its price will decrease; if it does, he can buy the bond back at a lower price and make a profit. Short positions have limited profit potential because the price of an asset cannot decrease below zero; however, they have unlimited loss potential because prices can increase infinitely. Many pension investors believe that shorting stocks is inappropriate for pension portfolios because ultimately doing so can be riskier than simply holding poor performers.

Standard Deviation: A measure of the mathematical deviation from the mean of two-thirds of a statistical sample. For example, assume the average annual return on the stocks of the S&P 500 were +15% and the standard deviation were +/- 15%. Given a normal distribution, two-thirds of the time the return of any stock chosen at random would fall between 0% and +30%. Standard deviation reflects the unpredictability of returns and is a useful indicator of risk, *to the extent that returns are normally distributed.*

Style: The investment strategies used by fund managers and /or mutual funds. Generally categorized by the three major asset classes (i.e., equity, fixed-income and money market), style incorporates all aspects of trading methodology, including asset types and sizes, investment analysis and duration. Examples of equity styles include "large-cap", which invests in stocks of companies with large-capitalization and "growth-style", which concentrates on stocks with higher-than-average earnings growth.

Swap: An over-the-counter derivative instrument used to change the characteristics of a portfolio. Originally, a swap referred to the simple exchange of one security for another; today, more complex swaps are being used, including currency swaps, interest rate swaps and swaps linked to mortgage-backed securities. In a typical interest rate swap, for example, two parties periodically exchange payments based upon the value of one or more market indices. Swaps can also provide leverage, since they require little or no initial capital outlay.

Swaptions: Options on interest rate swaps. Prior to the swaption's expiration date, the swaption holder has the right to enter into an interest rate swap with the swaption seller. The swaption agreement stipulates which party will receive the fixed rate of interest and which party will receive the floating rate, in the event the swaption is exercised.

Systems Risk: The risk that current system designs or implementations are inappropriate or ineffective to the extent that information obtained from or disseminated through the system environment is incorrect or incorrectly perceived and the decisions made based on that information is sub-optimal. In addition this includes the security of information in response to unauthorized access and disaster.

Tactical Asset Allocation: An asset allocation strategy which involves the relatively short-term process of making minor shifts within pre-established ranges.

Top-Down Investment Process: An investment strategy in which an investor first makes an assessment of overall economic indicators, and then decides which industries will profit most from economic conditions. The top-down investor then selects a portfolio of individual securities from within the favored industries.

Tracking Error: The differential in performance between a portfolio and its benchmark. Mathematically, it is the annualized standard deviation of the difference in return. In an indexing strategy, tracking error refers to the degree to which an index fund's performance diverges from its index.

Value-At-Risk (VAR): A statistical estimate of maximum potential loss that can be expected over a given period a certain percentage of the time. VAR is applied to complex portfolios as a way for financial organizations to sum up their total risk in a simple measure. It's an old concept built on the foundations of Modern Portfolio Theory, recently rediscovered in response to the rising interest in and need for risk measures and controls. How it is computed, its use and reliability are all the subject of considerable debate.

Volatility: A measure of the fluctuation in the price of a security, commodity or market. Mathematically, it is computed as the annualized standard deviation of the percentage change in daily price. A highly volatile security may experience wide price swings and is therefore considered to be more speculative than one with a low volatility.

APPENDIX

SUMMARY OF THE 20 RISK STANDARDS
Published by The Risk Standards Working Group, 1997

Note: Throughout this document, references to the "Primary Fiduciary" and/or "Manager Fiduciary" include their designees. References to the "Manager" include both the internal and the external investment manager.

I. MANAGEMENT
Risk Standard #1:

Acknowledgment of fiduciary responsibility
Fiduciary responsibilities should be defined in writing and acknowledged in writing by the parties responsible.

Risk Standard #2:
Approved written policies, definitions, guidelines and investment documentation
The Primary and Manager Fiduciaries should approve formal written policies which reflect their overall risk management objectives. The Primary Manager Fiduciaries also should approve investment guidelines, management agreements and all other contracts that govern investments. Technical terms should be defined. All policies, definition, guidelines and investment documentation should be reviewed and updated as appropriate and more often if significant market events or changes in strategy occur.

Risk Standard #3:
Independent risk oversight, checks and balances, written procedures and controls
Oversight of compliance with risk policies should be independent of line investment activity and conducted according to up-to-date, written policies and procedures. Front, middle, and back office activities should be separate wherever possible and sufficient checks and balances and appropriate controls should exist. When separation is not possible due to limited staff, alternative checks, balances and controls should be established.

Risk Standard #4:
Clearly defined organizational structure and key roles
Organizational structure and reporting lines should be defined clearly and distributed to all parties. Key personnel and their roles in all front, middle and back office areas should be identified. Changes in key personnel should be communicated immediately to all relevant parties.

Risk Standard #5:
Consistent application of risk policies
The Primary Fiduciary's risk policies should apply both to internal and external managers and should be consistent across similar asset classes and strategies.

Risk Standard #6:
Adequate education, systems and resources, back-up and disaster recovery plans
The Primary and Manager Fiduciaries should ensure that adequate education, systems and resources are available to implement and administer their risk policies. They should also establish and test back-up procedures and disaster recovery plans.

Risk Standard #7:
Identification and understanding of key risks
Risks should be analyzed to determine relevancy. This entails understanding strategies and their vulnerabilities, as well as assumptions built into an instrument, system, process, model or strategy. Key risks should be reviewed periodically as well as when significant events occur.

Risk Standard #8:
Setting risk limits
Risk limits should be set for the aggregate portfolio and all individual portfolios. These may include limits on asset classes, individual instruments and specific types of risk.

Risk Standard #9:
Routine reporting, exception reporting and escalation procedures
The Primary and Manager Fiduciaries should specify what positions, risks and other information must be reported and to whom. This policy also should define what constitutes required reporting or an exception to guidelines, to whom the exception should be reported, what action must be taken for different levels of violation and what procedures must be followed for ongoing or increased violations.

II. MEASUREMENT

Risk Standard #10:
Valuation procedures
All readily priced instruments should be valued daily, less-readily priced instruments at least weekly and non-readily priced instruments as often as feasible and whenever a material event occurs. The pricing mechanism and methodologies must be known, understood, follow written policies and be applied consistently by the Primary and Manager Fiduciaries, Managers, custodian and other subcontractors.

Risk Standard #11:
Valuation reconciliation, bid/offer adjustments and overrides
Material discrepancies in valuations from different sources should be reconciled following established procedures. A procedure for bid/offer adjustments and overrides to valuations should be established in writing and monitored independently.

Risk Standard #12:
Risk measurement and risk/return attribution analysis
The Primary and Manager Fiduciaries should regularly measure relevant risks and quantify the key drivers of risk and return.

Risk Standard #13:
Risk-adjusted return measures
Risk-adjusted returns should be measured at the aggregate and individual portfolio level to gain a true measure of relative performance.

Risk Standard #14:
Stress testing
Simulation or other stress tests should be performed to ascertain how the aggregate portfolio and individual portfolios would behave under various conditions. These include changes in key risk factors, correlations or other key assumptions and unusual events such as large market moves.

Risk Standard #15:
Back testing
Risk and return forecasts and models should be back tested at least quarterly and whenever material events occur to assess their reliability.

Risk Standard #16:
Assessing model risk
Dependence on models and assumptions for valuation, risk measurement and risk management should be evaluated and monitored.

III. OVERSIGHT

Risk Standard #17:
Due diligence, policy compliance and guideline monitoring
The Primary and Manager Fiduciaries should perform frequent, independent reviews of all Managers' risk policies and controls. Where policies and controls fall short of the requirements set forth by the Primary or Manager Fiduciaries, plans for future compliance or corrective action should be documented and communicated. Managers should ensure continuing compliance with their clients' risk policies and guidelines.

Risk Standard #18:
Comparison of Manager strategies to compensation and investment activity
The Primary Fiduciary should require each Manager to submit a statement of strategy and ensure that the Manager's activities and compensation are consistent with that strategy. Key risk and return factors should be documented and reviewed at least annually and updated whenever the strategy changes.

Risk Standard #19:
Independent review of methodologies, models and systems
All methodologies, models and related systems should be independently reviewed or audited prior to use as well as annually. Significant market moves or changes in market practice should trigger interim reviews.

Risk Standard #20:
Review process for new activities
The Primary and Manager Fiduciaries should document the review process for permitting the use of new instruments, strategies or asset classes. Policies for initiating new activities should be consistent with the Primary and Manager Fiduciaries' risk and return goals as well as the Manager's strategy and expertise.